WATERCOLOURS OF THE NORWICH SCHOOL

WATERCOLOURS OF

The Norwich School

by
DEREK CLIFFORD

CORY, ADAMS & MACKAY

First published 1965 by Cory, Adams & Mackay Ltd, 39 Sloane Street, London S.W.1.
The text is set in 'Monotype' Walbaum. Printed and bound by
W & J Mackay & Co Ltd, Chatham. Made in England.

Contents

Introduction   *page* 1

1. The Forerunners   3

2. First Period 1803–12   18

3. The Middle Period (a) 1812–24   35

4. The Middle Period (b) 1824–33   44

5. The Persisting Tradition   60

Appendices   81

Select Bibliography   88

COLOUR PLATES   *facing page*

I   The Mill Wheel   16

II   Timber Yard and Norwich Cathedral from the North   24

III   The Mill, Eye, Suffolk   32

IV   Snowdon from Capel Curig   40

V   Dreadnought and Grampus, Hospital Ships on the Thames   48

VI   A Barn   56

VII   River Landscape   64

VIII   Alby, Norfolk   72

MONOCHROME REPRODUCTIONS   93

List of Illustrations

COLOUR PLATES

I
John Crome (1768–1821).
The Mill Wheel 11½ × 16¼ in.
Indistinctly signed bottom left.
MR AND MRS D. P. CLIFFORD.
A 'Water Mill near Lynn' was sold by Messrs.
Spelman in 1872. There were a number of
water-mills in the Lynn neighbourhood. If this
drawing is the one sold in 1872
the subject may be the mill at West Norton.

II
John Thirtle (1777–1839).
*Timber Yard and Norwich Cathedral from the
North* 9½ × 13¼ in.
Signed and dated: *J. Thirtle, 1829.*
G. ALLEN.
Ex collection: Thirkettle.

III
John Sell Cotman (1782–1842).
The Mill, Eye, Suffolk 8⅛ × 12⅜ in.
CASTLE MUSEUM, NORWICH.
Ex collection: R. J. Colman.
A pencil drawing for this is in
The National Gallery, Washington.

IV
Robert Leman (1799–1863).
Snowdon from Capel Curig 12¾ × 19⅞ in.
CASTLE MUSEUM, NORWICH.
Ex collection: R. J. Colman; bought by J. Reeve at
the artists' sale, 1863.
Exhibited: Norwich 1927 as 'View on the Greta'
(No. 197).

V
Miles Edmund Cotman (1810–1858).
*Dreadnought and Grampus, Hospital Ships on the
Thames* 16⅝ × 22⅜ in.
Signed and dated: *M. E. Cotman 1830* also
initialled *M.E.C.* on ship.
ALEC COTMAN.
Lit.: Barnard, *Paintings of the Norwich School*;
Norwich School Loan Exhibition 1927 (149).
Exhibited: probably at Norwich, 1833; Burlington
Fine Arts Club, 1886; Norwich, 1927 (149).

VI
Henry Bright (1810–1873).
A Barn 15 × 20 in.
Signed: *H. Bright.*
G. ALLEN.

VII
John Joseph Cotman (1814–1878).
River Landscape 12⅜ × 18⅜ in.
ALEC COTMAN.
Ex collection: 'Mr Cooper', who bought it from
the artist.
Exhibited: *Art of the Seven Cotmans*, Norwich,
1942.

VIII
John Middleton (1827–1856).
Alby, Norfolk 12⅞ × 19 in.
Signed and dated: *J.M.* monogram, *Alby,
Norfolk*, 1847.
CASTLE MUSEUM, NORWICH.
Ex collection: R. J. Colman.
Lit.: *John Middleton. A sketch of His Life and
Work* by Francis W. Hawcroft, p. 4.

MONOCHROME REPRODUCTIONS

1a
John Ninham (1754–1817).
A View of Norwich 9½ × 19½ in.
CASTLE MUSEUM, NORWICH.
Ex collection: Revd J. Bulwer.
Lit.: *Cot. and Haw, p. 14*, pl. 5.
There is an oil painting of the same view at
Norwich.

1b
Attributed to Charles Catton R.A. (1728–1798).
A View of the Bridges at Hawick 15⅞ × 23 9/16 in.
VICTORIA AND ALBERT MUSEUM.

2a
Charles Catton, Junior (1756–1819).
*A View of Norwich from Mousehold Heath, near
the Ruins of Ketts Castle* 4 × 6 7/16 in.
VICTORIA AND ALBERT MUSEUM.

2b
William Capon (1757–1827).
*The Entrance to the Opera House, Haymarket, as
Built by Vanbrugh* 7⅜ × 9⅛ in.
1783.
BRITISH MUSEUM.
Ex collection: Crace.
Lit.: Winton Dean, *Handel's Dramatic Oratories
and Masques*, pl. 1a.

3a
William Williams (fl. 1758–1795).
Vagrants With a Donkey 11 1/16 × 16¾ in.
Signed and dated: *W. Williams, 1795.*
VICTORIA AND ALBERT MUSEUM.

3b
William Williams (fl. 1758–1795).
Loading a Pack Donkey 10¾ × 14¾ in.
Signed and dated: *W. Williams, 1795.*
CASTLE MUSEUM, NORWICH.

4a
James Sillett (1764–1840).
Black Grapes 19¼ × 13 in.
Signed: *J. Sillett.*
CASTLE MUSEUM, NORWICH.
Ex collection: Mrs Blyth.

4b
James Sillett (1764–1840).
The Old Oak at Winfarthing 8 × 11⅝ in.
CASTLE MUSEUM, NORWICH.
Ex collection: Revd J. Bulwer.

5a
Attributed to James Sillett (1770–1842).
Bishop's Bridge, Norwich 10⅜ × 16⅛ in.
CASTLE MUSEUM, NORWICH.
Ex collection: Revd James Bulwer.

5b
Charles Hodgson (fl. 1797).
River Scene, gouache, 12 × 16 in.
CASTLE MUSEUM, NORWICH.
Ex collection: Sir Henry Holmes.

6a
John Crome (1768–1821).
Near Lakenham 5 × 10½ in.
CASTLE MUSEUM, NORWICH.
Ex collection: R. Dixon; Sir Henry Studdy
Theobald; J. Reeve; R. J. Colman.
Lit.: *Cundall*, pl. 27.
Exhibited: Norwich, 1903; Crome Centenary,
1921 (69).

6b
John Crome (1768–1821).
?*Patterdale*, Grey wash, 8½ × 12½ in.
c. 1802.
FITZWILLIAM MUSEUM, CAMBRIDGE.
Formerly attributed to J. S. Cotman but
undoubtedly Crome and probably the drawing
entitled PATTERDALE: SKETCH IN INDIAN
INK exhibited at Norwich in 1805.

7a
John Crome (1768–1821).
Tintern Abbey 19 × 14¾ in.
c. 1805.
CASTLE MUSEUM, NORWICH.
Ex collection: R. J. Colman.

7b
John Crome (1768–1821).
By the Roadside 10¼ × 8¼ in.
c. 1801.

WHITWORTH ART GALLERY, MANCHESTER.
Exhibited: Crome Centenary, 1921 (81);
Arts Council, 1948;
Loan Exhibition, Agnew, 1954 (41).

8a
John Crome (1768–1821).
Mountainous Landscape $6\frac{15}{16} \times 10\frac{15}{16}$ in.
c. 1801.
L. G. DUKE.
Ex collection: James Ward, R.A.

8b
John Crome (1768–1821).
Trees on a Bank, grey wash, $11\frac{1}{5} \times 16\frac{3}{8}$ in.
BRITISH MUSEUM.
Said to be trees between St Martin's Gate and Hillesden.

9a
John Crome (1768–1821).
The River Through the Trees $13\frac{7}{8} \times 18$ in.
c. 1802.
SIR EDMUND BACON, BART.
Lit.: *Iolo Williams, 154.*

9b
John Crome (1768–1821).
The Sunken Lane $7\frac{7}{8} \times 12\frac{3}{4}$ in.
BRITISH MUSEUM.
Lit.: *Cundall.* pl. XXIX.

10a
John Crome (1768–1821).
Entrance to Earlham Park $22\frac{1}{4} \times 18\frac{1}{8}$ in.
MR AND MRS PAUL MELLON.
Lit.: *Apollo*, Vol. LXXVII, No. 14, April 1963, ill.
Exhibited: Washington, National Gallery of Art, 1962, (26); Richmond, Virginia, 1963 (167); London, Colnaghi, 1964 (47).

10b
John Crome (1768–1821).
Blacksmith's Shop at Hingham $15\frac{1}{4} \times 11\frac{1}{2}$ in.
MUSEUM AND ART GALLERY, DONCASTER.
Ex collection: W. W. Spelman; Waterhouse family; Miss Ethel Colman.
Lit.: *Baker, p. 122*, pl. IX; F. W. Hawcroft. *Connoisseur*, Dec. 1959.
Exhibited: Crome Centenary, 1921 (83); Sheffield, Graves Art Gallery, 1952; Manchester, Whitworth Art Gallery, 1961 (34).
Two versions of *A Blacksmith's Shop from Nature* were exhibited at the Norwich Society, 1807.
An oil of this subject now in The Philadelphia Museum was exhibited in the R.A. in 1808.

11a
John Crome (1768–1821).
The Blasted Oak $23 \times 17\frac{1}{4}$ in.
SIR EDMUND BACON, BART.
Lit.: *Iolo Williams 153, 154.*
Exhibited: Arts Council, 1946 (54); Arts Council, 1951 (57); Norwich, 1955 (30); Geneva and Zurich, 1955–6 (50); Manchester, Whitworth Art Gallery (pl. 38) 1961.

11b
John Crome (1768–1821).
The Glade Cottage $25 \times 21\frac{3}{4}$ in.
THE VISCOUNT MACKINTOSH OF HALIFAX.
Ex collection: Bignold.

12
John Crome (1768–1821).
Wood Scene $22\frac{1}{4} \times 16\frac{1}{4}$ in.
VICTORIA AND ALBERT MUSEUM.
Lit.: *Iolo Williams, p. 154*; *Cundall*, pl. 26; Dickes, p. 147.
Baker, who calls it *Grove Scene? Lake in Distance* suggests it may have been shown at Norwich, 1809 and The British Institute, 1850; also perhaps The Society of Arts, 1861.
Another version, *A Lane near Norwich*, is at Norwich Castle.

13
John Crome (1768–1821).
Houses and Wherries on the Wensum $11\frac{3}{4} \times 15\frac{5}{8}$ in.
c. 1813.
WHITWORTH ART GALLERY, MANCHESTER.
Lit.: *Iolo Williams, p. 156.*
Exhibited: Huddersfield, 1946; Agnews, 1954 (40) Arts Council, 1960 (28); Manchester, Whitworth Art Gallery, 1961 (39).
Formerly catalogued as *Houses and Wherries on the Yare*. Another later version is in the City Art Gallery, Manchester (*Baker*, pl. LII).
F. W. Hawcroft suggests it is by a close follower.

14a
John Crome (1768–1821).
Silver Birches $9\frac{3}{4} \times 7\frac{7}{8}$ in.
Signed: *J. Crome.*
1814.

CASTLE MUSEUM, NORWICH.
Ex collection: R. J. Colman.
Lit.: Hawcroft, *Connoisseur, Dec. 1959, p. 236,*
pl. 12.
Exhibited: Kettering, 1952 (19); Kidderminster,
1954; Derby and Nottingham, 1959 (31);
Manchester, Whitworth, 1961.
Copied from *Landscape with Sportsman and Game*
by Adam Pynacker (1622–1673) in the Dulwich
Gallery. Dulwich was opened in 1814 and the copy
is likely to have been made by Crome on his
journey to France in that year.

14b
John Crome (1768–1821).
Trees by Water 10⅛ × 11½ in.
1814.
MR AND MRS D. P. CLIFFORD.
Copied from the centre of *Evening Ride near a
River* by Cuyp in the Dulwich Gallery. Technically
related to Plate 14a.

15a
Attributed to Robert Ladbrooke (1770–1842).
The Waggoner and Oak 12½ × 19¼ in.
Grey, heightened with white, on blue paper.
MR AND MRS D. P. CLIFFORD.

15b
Robert Ladbrooke (1770–1842).
Norfolk Broad, Evening 8½ × 11 in.
MR AND MRS CYRIL FRY.

16
Robert Ladbrooke (1770–1842).
A Forge by Moonlight 10 × 13½ in.
MR AND MRS D. P. CLIFFORD.

17a
Robert Ladbrooke (1770–1842).
Glymllffes Bridge, North Wales 21½ × 15¾ in.
c. 1803.
Inscribed with title low left; and on the back by
James Reeve as having been bought at J. B.
Ladbrooke's sale.
CASTLE MUSEUM, NORWICH.

17b
John Thirtle (1777–1839).
Harvest Time 16⅜ × 12¾ in.
CASTLE MUSEUM, NORWICH.
Possibly after Westall.

18a
John Thirtle (1777–1839).
Beached Fishing Boat 9 × 9¾ in.
G. ALLEN.
Ex collection: Blofeld.

18b
John Thirtle (1777–1839).
Thorpe Staithe 9¾ × 13¼ in.
CASTLE MUSEUM, NORWICH.
Ex collection: J. B. Aldis.
Exhibited: Thirtle Exhibition, 1886, ill.

19a
John Thirtle (1777–1839).
Tombland, Norwich 13½ × 21¼ in.
CASTLE MUSEUM, NORWICH.
Ex collection: Thirkettle.
Lit.: *Studio, Aug. 1947, p. 30.*
Exhibited: Norwich, 1927 (282); Norwich, 1939
(35); Kidderminster, 1954; Worthing, 1957
(32); Derby and Nottingham, 1959 (61);
Whitworth, 1961 (42).
A similar view was formerly in the collection of
Dean Cranage.

19b
John Thirtle (1777–1839).
River Scene Near Norwich 8 × 11¼ in.
CASTLE MUSEUM, NORWICH.

20
John Thirtle (1777–1839).
View Over a Plain 8⅞ × 14¼ in.
VICTORIA AND ALBERT MUSEUM.

21a
Edwin W. Cooper (fl. 1803–*c.* 1833).
A Piebald Horse and a Dog in a Landscape.
9¾ × 12 in.
Signed and dated: *E. W. Cooper, 1803.*
MR AND MRS D. P. CLIFFORD.
One of a pair.

21b
Edwin W. Cooper (fl. 1803–*c.* 1833).
A House in a Park 12 × 15½ in.
MR AND MRS D. P. CLIFFORD.

22a
J. Gooch (fl. 1797–1833).
Beaudesert 5½ × 8¾ in.
Signed and dated: *J. Gooch 1797* and inscribed
with title on back.
MR AND MRS D. P. CLIFFORD.

22b
J. Gooch (fl. 1797–1833).
Old Carrow Bridge 13 × 19¼ in.
After 1810.
CASTLE MUSEUM, NORWICH.
Ex collection: Revd. J. Bulwer.
Lit.: *Cot. and Haw.*, p. 15, pl. 7.
Formerly attribted to John Ninham. This bridge was built in 1810.

23a
Major-General James Pattison Cockburn (1779–1847).
Cavalry Barracks, Norwich 9⅛ × 17½ in.
CASTLE MUSEUM, NORWICH.
Ex collection: Revd J. Bulwer.

23b
Robert Dixon (1780–1815).
Cottage Scene 13 × 21½ in.
Signed: *R. Dixon.*
G. ALLEN.

24a
Robert Dixon (1780–1815).
Village Windmill 4⅜ × 9¼ in.
BRITISH MUSEUM.
Ex collection: James Reeve.

24b
Robert Dixon (1780–1815).
The Mill at Cromer 7 × 9¾ in.
CASTLE MUSEUM, NORWICH.
Ex collection: R. J. Colman.
Exhibited: Norwich, 1927 (176).

25a
Robert Dixon (1780–1815).
Fishermen's Cottages, Overstrand Near Cromer, Morning 5⅞ × 9½ in.
Inscribed with title low left.
BRITISH MUSEUM.
Ex collection: Arthur Dixon; James Reeve.
Lit.: *Iolo Williams, p. 156.*

25b
Robert Dixon (1780–1815).
Beeston Hill, Sheringham in the Distance. 6¼ × 12 in.
CASTLE MUSEUM, NORWICH.
Ex collection: R. J. Colman.
Exhibited: Norwich, 1927 (175).

26a
Paul Sandby Munn (1775–1845).
Mill on the Vale of Rhyddal, Cardiganshire 12¾ × 9⅝ in.
Signed and dated: *P. S. Munn, 1807,* inscribed with title on the back.
MR AND MRS D. P. CLIFFORD.
Ex collection: C. E. Preston.

26b
Francis Stevens (1781–1823).
House at Wortley, nr. Sheffield 18 × 14¾ in.
Signed: *F. Stevens.*
VICTORIA AND ALBERT MUSEUM.

27a
Francis Stevens (1781–1823).
Near Beccles, Suffolk 18⅞ × 11⅞ in.
Inscribed with title.
DR AND MRS D. KIRKHAM.

27b
Attributed to David Cox (1783–1859).
Evening Landscape 5¼ × 9¼ in.
c. 1809.
MR AND MRS D. P. CLIFFORD.

28a
John Sell Cotman (1782–1842).
Cottage Near Guildford Churchyard 14 × 20¾ in.
Signed and dated: *J. S. Cotman, 1800,* and inscribed on reverse: *14 March 1800.*
NOTTINGHAM CITY ART GALLERY.
Exhibited: Royal Academy, 1800.

28b
John Sell Cotman (1782–1842).
Brecknock 14⅞ × 21½ in.
Inscribed on back: *Brecknock, S. Wales, Cotman.*
c. 1801.
SIR EDMUND BACON, BART.
Lit.: *Dickes, p. 252; Kitson, p. 25.*
Exhibited: Royal Academy, 1801 (311); Hull, 1938 (1); Arts Council, 1946 (27); Agnew, 1946; Royal Academy, 1951–2 (485); Norwich, 1955 (52); Manchester, Whitworth Art Gallery, 1961.

29a
John Sell Cotman (1782–1842).
Barmouth Estuary 6¹³⁄₁₆ × 11¼ in.
Signed and dated: *J. S. Cotman, 1801.*
CASTLE MUSEUM, NORWICH.
Ex collection: R. J. Colman.
Lit.: Rienaecker, pl. 14.

29b
John Sell Cotman (1782–1842).
Bedlam Furnace 10¼ × 18¾ in.
c. 1801.
SIR EDMUND BACON, BART.
Lit.: *Kitson, p. 41,* pl. 5; *Oppé, p. viii.*
Exhibited: Hull, 1938 (4); Arts Council, 1946 (25);
(25); Norwich, 1955 (51); Manchester,
Whitworth, 1961 (46).

30a
John Sell Cotman (1782–1842).
An Overshot Mill 18⅞ × 14 in.
c. 1800.
FITZWILLIAM MUSEUM, CAMBRIDGE.
Ex collection: Lord Ivor Spencer Churchill.
Exhibited: Royal Academy, 1800, as *A Water
Mill Near Dorking.*
Perhaps the drawing for which 'The larger Silver
Palette' was awarded by *The Society for the
Encouragement of Arts.*

30b
John Sell Cotman (1782–1842).
Study of Trees, Harrow 14½ × 11 in.
Inscribed low right: *July* (?) 1805 and left:
Harrow. Mr D. E. Cox.
WHITWORTH ART GALLERY, MANCHESTER.
Lit.: *Kitson, p. 77;* Old Water Colour Society's
Club, 1939, pl. XX.

31a
John Sell Cotman (1782–1842).
Devil's Elbow, Rokeby Park 17¾ × 13⅞ in.
c. 1806.
CASTLE MUSEUM, NORWICH.
Ex collection: R. J. Colman.
Lit.: *Kitson,* pl. 35; *Barnard,* pl. 14; *Guide to
Colman Collection, p. 6; Rienaecker,* pl. 20.

31b
John Sell Cotman (1782–1842).
Ancient Bath, Composition 17¾ × 13 in.
c. 1807.
MR AND MRS CYRIL FRY.
Exhibited: Norwich, 1807 (9).

32a
John Sell Cotman (1782–1842).
The Mars riding at anchor off Cromer (12 × 8⅝ in.
c. 1807.
CASTLE MUSEUM, NORWICH.
Lit.: *Kitson, 111, 112, 127, 179,* pl. 48.
Ex collection: R. J. Colman.

32b
John Sell Cotman (1782–1842).
The Marl Pit 11⅝ × 10⅛ in.
c. 1809.
CASTLE MUSEUM, NORWICH.
Ex collection: R. J. Colman.
Lit.: *Guide to Colman Collection, p. 10; Kitson,
p. 122.*

33a
John Sell Cotman (1782–1842).
St Botolph's Priory, Colchester 14 × 20½ in.
c. 1808.
CASTLE MUSEUM, NORWICH.
Ex collection: James Orrock; R. J. Colman.
There is a smaller version in the Lupton
Collection.
Lit.: *Kitson, 67, 145,* pl. 26; *Rienaecker,* pl. 16.

33b
John Sell Cotman (1782–1842).
Cottages, Elm Hill, Norwich 10¾ × 15½ in.
1809.
CASTLE MUSEUM, NORWICH.
Ex collection: R. J. Colman.

34a
John Sell Cotman (1782–1842).
A Castle 8¾ × 13 in.
c. 1809.
CASTLE MUSEUM, NORWICH.
Ex collection: R. J. Colman.

34b
John Sell Cotman (1782–1842).
St Paul's from the River 7¾ × 12¾ in
c. 1801.
BRITISH MUSEUM.
Ex collection: Dawson Turner.

35a
John Sell Cotman (1782–1842).
Boston Church, Lincs. 8 × 10½ in.
1805.
Inscribed on back: *1805, Boston, Lincs. J.S.C.*
MR AND MRS D. P. CLIFFORD.

35b
John Sell Cotman (1782–1842).
Coutances 10½ × 17¾ in.
1820.
CASTLE MUSEUM, NORWICH.
Ex collection: R. J. Colman.

36a
John Sell Cotman (1782–1842).
Abbatial House of St Ouen, Rouen 16¼ × 22¼ in.
Signed and dated: *J. S. Cotman, 1825.*
CASTLE MUSEUM, NORWICH.
Ex collection: R. J. Colman.
Lit.: *Kitson 257, 258, 262,* pl. 113; *Dickes, p. 339;
Norwich Art Circle Catalogue,* 1888; Rienaecker,
pl. 81.
Exhibited: Norwich Art Circle, 1888 (164) ill.;
Old Masters, 1892.
There are at least four versions of this drawing.
The first water-colour version was exhibited at
Norwich in 1824 and is now in the V. and A. A
replica was exhibited with the Old Water Colour
Society in 1831. The house was taken down in
1817. Cotman was at Rouen in that year.

36b
John Sell Cotman (1782–1842).
*Snowdon with the Lake of Llanberis, near
Dolbadern Castle* 20 × 28½ in.
1824.
THE VISCOUNT MACKINTOSH OF HALIFAX.
Ex collection: Revd James Bulwer.
Lit.: *Kitson, 258, Dickes, 347;* Rienaecker, pl. 11.
Exhibited: Norwich, 1824; Norwich Art Circle,
1888 (34) as 'Lake Scene in Westmorland';
Harrowgate, 1953; Fitzwilliam, 1958.
Lord Mackintosh also owns the original pencil
sketch.

37a
John Sell Cotman (1782–1842).
Mills at Crowland 10¼ × 7½ in.
Inscribed on back in the artist's hand: *Crowland,
Lincolnshire, J. S. Cotman No. 5.*
c. 1824.
MR AND MRS D. P. CLIFFORD.
This is one of several variants of a drawing made
at Croyland in 1804 (Kitson, p. 73); see also pl.
37b; pl. 79 in V. & A. Catalogue, 1927; and
Hughes, 1950, pl. 35.

37b
John Sell Cotman (1782–1842).
A Draining Mill 20¾ × 14⅞ in.
c. 1831.
SIR EDMUND BACON, BART.
See note to pl. 37a.

38a
John Sell Cotman (1782–1842).
Storm on Yarmouth Beach 14⅜ × 21 in.
Signed and dated: *J. S. Cotman, 1831.*

CASTLE MUSEUM, NORWICH.
Ex collection: G. Holmes.
Lit.: *Norwich Arts Circle Catalogue, 1880, No.
167;* Dickes, p. 372; Kitson, pl. 27; Barnard, pl. 15.
Exhibited: Water Colour Society, 1831; Norwich
Arts Circle, 1880 (167) ill.

38b
John Sell Cotman (1782–1842).
*Landscape Composition with the Story of
Bathsheba* 13¾ × 18 in.
Signed: *J. S. Cotman, 1833.*
CASTLE MUSEUM, NORWICH.
Ex collection: R. J. Colman.
Lit.: *Kitson, 299.*
Exhibited: Norwich, 1833.

39a
John Sell Cotman (1782–1842).
Via Mala 15¾ × 12 in.
1829.
CASTLE MUSEUM, NORWICH.
Ex collection: R. J. Colman.
Lit.: *Kitson, 285; Dickes, 362.*
Exhibited: Manchester, 1887.
After a sketch by Joseph Geldart; related
drawings are in the collection of Lord
Mackintosh, *Rienaecker,* pl. 49; and *Norwich
Art Circle Catalogue,* 1888.

39b
John Sell Cotman (1782–1842).
The Wind in the Trees 16 × 11 7/16 in.
c. 1833.
CASTLE MUSEUM, NORWICH.
Ex collection: R. J. Colman.

40a
John Sell Cotman (1782–1842).
Mountain Landscape 8 × 11¾ in.
c. 1835.
BRITISH MUSEUM.
Ex collection: James Reeve.

40b
John Sell Cotman (1782–1842).
Trees on a Hill 8⅝ × 13⅝ in.
c. 1840.
CASTLE MUSEUM, NORWICH.
Ex collection: R. J. Colman.
Lit.: *Cundall,* pl. XLVII.

41a
David Cox (1783–1859).
The Windmill, grey wash, 6⅞ × 8⅞ in.
c. 1810.
MR AND MRS D. P. CLIFFORD.

41b
Attributed to Edmund Girling (1796–1871)
or
Richard Girling (1799–1863).
Cumberland $13\frac{3}{4} \times 19\frac{1}{4}$ in.
CASTLE MUSEUM, NORWICH.

42a
Henry Ninham (1793–1874).
St Andrew's, Norwich, 1848 $6\frac{7}{8} \times 5\frac{1}{4}$ in.
CASTLE MUSEUM, NORWICH.

42b
Henry Ninham (1793–1874).
A Thatched Cottage $9\frac{1}{8} \times 11\frac{3}{16}$ in.
BRITISH MUSEUM.
Ex collection: James Reeve.

43a
John Berney Crome (1794–1842).
Yarmouth Beach with Windmills $5\frac{5}{8} \times 9\frac{1}{8}$ in.
CASTLE MUSEUM, NORWICH.
Ex collection: Revd J. Bulwer.

43b
John Berney Crome (1794–1842).
Yarmouth Beach, 1840 $6 \times 13\frac{3}{4}$ in.
Inscribed on the back: *Yarmouth Beach June 1st, 1840 To Henry Penrice from John Berney Crome.*
PUBLIC LIBRARY, GREAT YARMOUTH.
There is a copy in the same collection by Miss Cecilia Lucy Brightwell.

44a
James Stark (1794–1859).
In the Isle of Purbeck $8\frac{3}{4} \times 11\frac{7}{8}$ in.
S. ROWLAND PIERCE.
Ex collection: G. Birkbeck.
Exhibited: Arts Club, London, 1959; Brighton, 1962.

44b
James Stark (1794–1859).
Eton College $9\frac{5}{8} \times 14$ in.
CASTLE MUSEUM, NORWICH.
Ex collection: R. J. Colman.

45a
James Stark (1794–1859).
Sandhills on the Coast at Winterton, Norfolk $8\frac{5}{8} \times 12\frac{15}{16}$ in.
VICTORIA AND ALBERT MUSEUM.

45b
James Stark (1794–1859).
Cottages $7\frac{1}{4} \times 10\frac{3}{8}$ in.
VICTORIA AND ALBERT MUSEUM.

46a
James Stark (1794–1859).
The Pasture Pond $9\frac{3}{4} \times 13\frac{3}{4}$ in.
VICTORIA AND ALBERT MUSEUM.

46b
James Stark (1794–1859).
Rocks and Trees $9 \times 13\frac{1}{4}$ in.
CASTLE MUSEUM, NORWICH.

47a
James Bulwer (1794–1879).
Near Clifton $8\frac{1}{4} \times 13\frac{3}{4}$ in.
Dated: *June 18/1831.*
CASTLE MUSEUM, NORWICH.
Ex collection: Revd J. Bulwer.

47b
James Bulwer (1794–1879).
Beeston Regis Church $5\frac{7}{8} \times 8\frac{1}{8}$ in.
CASTLE MUSEUM, NORWICH.
Ex collection: Revd J. Bulwer.

48a
George Vincent (1796–1832).
The Needles $6\frac{1}{2} \times 8$ in.
Signed and dated: *G V monogram 1830.*
CASTLE MUSEUM, NORWICH.
Exhibited: Society of British Artists, 1832.

48b
George Vincent (1796–1832).
Shipping Scene $6\frac{1}{4} \times 9\frac{1}{4}$ in.
CASTLE MUSEUM, NORWICH.
Ex collection: R. J. Colman.
Formerly attributed to Joseph Stannard.

49a
George Vincent (1796–1832).
In the Highlands 10×14 in.
Signed and dated: *G V monogram 1830.*
H. DAY.

49b
George Vincent (1796–1832).
Prospect from a Ruin $10\frac{1}{2} \times 16$ in.
MR AND MRS D. P. CLIFFORD.

50
Joseph Stannard (1797–1830).
Lugger in a Squall, gouche, 10 × 14 in.
Signed: *J S monogram.*
MR AND MRS D. P. CLIFFORD.

51a
Joseph Stannard (1797–1830).
Schooners in a Calm Sea 7⅝ × 10⅞ in.
S. ROWLAND PIERCE.
Exhibited: Architectural Association, 1950;
Brighton, 1962.

51b
Joseph Stannard (1797–1830).
Hoisting the Sail 11 11/16 × 17 5/16 in.
CASTLE MUSEUM, NORWICH.

52a
William Joy (1803–1867)
and
John Cantiloe Joy (1806–1866).
*Shipping and Boats: King George IV passing Great
Ormseby, Yarmouth, on his return from
Edinburgh, 1822.*
11½ × 18⅜ in.
VICTORIA AND ALBERT MUSEUM.

52b
J. G. Zobell (Fl. 1819).
Sandling Ferry 9½ × 14½ in.
MR AND MRS D. P. CLIFFORD.

53a
David Hodgson (1798–1864).
Horstead Mills 7⅜ × 11⅞ in.
Signed and dated: *Horstead Mills, D.H.
August 1816.*
CASTLE MUSEUM, NORWICH.
Ex collection: R. J. Colman.

53b
David Hodgson (1798–1864).
Landscape with Trees 9⅝ × 13½ in.
CASTLE MUSEUM, NORWICH.
Ex collection: Mrs F. H. S. Hodgson.

54a
Thomas Churchyard (1798–1865).
The Moored Barge 7¾ × 11½ in.
BRITISH MUSEUM.

54b
Samuel David Colkett (1800–1863).
Cottage Scene 4½ × 6¼ in.
Signed and dated: *S. D. Colkett 1832.*
G. ALLEN.

55a
Samuel David Colkett (1800–1863).
The Track to the Field 5¾ × 7¾ in.
MR AND MRS D. P. CLIFFORD.

55b
Samuel David Colkett (1800–1863).
The Woodland Cottage 9 × 13 in.
MR AND MRS D. P. CLIFFORD.
There is a sepia pen over pencil drawing of the
same scene on the back.

56a
Robert Leman (1799–1863).
Cattle in a Pool 14½ × 11 in.
MR AND MRS D. P. CLIFFORD

56b
Robert Leman (1799–1863).
Trees 12½ × 9¾ in.
A. FELLOWS.

57
Robert Leman (1799–1863).
The Water Gate 8½ × 15¾ in.
BRITISH MUSEUM.
Ex collection: James Reeve.

58a
Robert Leman (1799–1863).
The Shepherd on the Heath 7⅜ × 11 in.
CASTLE MUSEUM, NORWICH.
Exhibited: Norwich, 1927 (195).

58b
Robert Leman (1799–1863).
At Trowse 9 11/16 × 13¼ in.
CASTLE MUSEUM, NORWICH.
Ex collection: R. J. Colman.

59a
G. S. Stevenson (Fl. 1830).
The Old Fishmarket 4¾ × 6½ in.
CASTLE MUSEUM, NORWICH.

59b
William Taylor (1800–1861).
Purfleet 10¼ × 8 in.
CASTLE MUSEUM, NORWICH.

60a
Thomas Lound (1802–1861).
Gorleston Pier 5¼ × 8 15/16 in.
CASTLE MUSEUM, NORWICH.
Ex collection: R. J. Colman.

60b
Thomas Lound (1802–1861).
View of Norwich 5¾ × 9 in.
CASTLE MUSEUM, NORWICH.

61a
Thomas Lound (1802–1861).
Boathouse on the Yare at Reedham 12 × 18½ in.
G. ALLEN.
Ex collection: Thirkettle.

61b
Thomas Lound (1802–1861).
Cottages at East Barsham, Norfolk 9 3/16 × 12⅞ in.
CASTLE MUSEUM, NORWICH.

62a
Thomas Lound (1802–1861).
St Benet's Abbey 9¼ × 16½ in.
G. ALLEN.
Ex collection: Thirkettle.

62b
John Berney Ladbrooke (1803–1879).
Below Beddgelert 9 × 13 in.
Signed and dated: *J. B. Ladbrooke, 1852*.
G. ALLEN.
Ex collection: Shaw Tomkin.

63a
John Berney Ladbrooke (1803–1879).
View in Snowdonia 8 × 14 in.
G. ALLEN.

63b
Attributed to John Berney Ladbrooke (1803–1879).
or
George Vincent (1796–1832).
The Team at the Bridge 12⅛ × 9¾ in.
CASTLE MUSEUM, NORWICH.
Ex collection: S. D. Kitson.

64a
Obadiah Short (1803–1886).
Norwich from Mousehold 5¼ × 8⅜ in.
CASTLE MUSEUM, NORWICH.

64b
Edward Thomas Daniell (1804–1842).
River Scene 5½ × 10¾ in.
BRITISH MUSEUM.
Exhibited: Norwich, 1927 (169).

65a
Edward Thomas Daniell (1804–1842).
Stormy Sunset 7⅝ × 13 in.
BRITISH MUSEUM.
Ex collection: James Reeve.
Exhibited: Norwich, 1927 (168).

65b
Edward Thomas Daniell (1804–1842).
Near Kalabshee 10 × 13¾ in.
Inscribed with title and date: *30th March 1841*.
CASTLE MUSEUM, NORWICH.
Ex collection: R. J. Colman.

66
Edward Thomas Daniell (1804–1842).
El Fatha, Sinai 9¾ × 13⅝ in.
Inscribed with title and date: *1841*.
CASTLE MUSEUM, NORWICH.
Ex collection: R. J. Colman.

67a
William Howes Hunt (1807–1879).
Yarmouth 18 × 27½ in.
Signed and dated: *W. H. Hunt 1861 (or '41)*.
CENTRAL LIBRARY, GREAT YARMOUTH.
There is a similar view by T. Lound at
Norwich Castle.

67b
Alfred Priest (1810–1850).
River Scene 6¼ × 10¼ in.
Signed: *Priest*, and said in Colman Catalogue to
be dated *1833*.
CASTLE MUSEUM, NORWICH.
Ex collection: R. J. Colman.

68a
Joseph Geldart (1803–1882).
Landscape Composition 10¾ × 13½ in.
Charcoal and wash.
CASTLE MUSEUM, NORWICH.
Exhibited: Norwich, 1927 (184).

68b
Attributed to Joseph Geldart (1803–1882).
The Well 10½ × 14¾ in.
Charcoal and wash.
SIR EDMUND BACON, BART.
Formely attributed to John Crome or to S. W.
Reynolds.

69a
Miles Edmund Cotman (1810–1858).
Interior of a Barn 15⅛ × 10⅞ in.

CASTLE MUSEUM, NORWICH.
There is a pencil drawing for this at Norwich Castle.

69b
Miles Edmund Cotman (1810–1858).
On the Bank of the Yare, Reedham 5 × 7½ in.
G. ALLEN.
Based on a chalk drawing by John Sell Cotman, formerly in the Theobald Collection.

70a
Miles Edmund Cotman (1810–1858).
A River Bank 7 × 10⅜ in.
BRITISH MUSEUM.
Ex collection: James Reeve.

70b
William Philip Barnes Freeman (1813–1897).
Breydon 12⅞ × 18⅞ in.
CASTLE MUSEUM, NORWICH.

71a
William Philip Barnes Freeman (1813–1897).
The Village Pump 6½ × 9½ in.
DR P. A. TYSER.
Formerly attributed to S. D. Colkett.

71b
Henry Bright (1814–1873).
Sunset at Low Tide 8¼ × 13½ in.
BRITISH MUSEUM.

72a
Henry Bright (1814–1873).
Low Tide 12⅞ × 18⅝ in.
Signed and dated: *H. Bright, 1841.*
VICTORIA AND ALBERT MUSEUM.

72b
Henry Bright (1814–1873).
Windmill by a River 13 × 20 in.
Signed and dated: *H. Bright, 1859.*
MR AND MRS D. P. CLIFFORD.

73a
Henry Bright (1814–1873).
Old Mill Clovelly, N. Devon 14¼ × 12 in.
Signed and dated on left: *H. Bright 1841*, and on right: *H. Bright.*
MR AND MRS D. P. CLIFFORD.
Exhibited: New Society of Painters in Water-Colour, 1841.

73b
John Joseph Cotman (1814–1873).
The Dolphin Inn, River Wensum 14 × 26 in.
DR JOHN SELL COTMAN.

74
John Joseph Cotman (1814–1873).
Foliage, Late Summer 14½ × 20 in.
Signed and dated: *J. J. Cotman, 1870.*
DR JOHN SELL COTMAN.

75a
John Joseph Cotman (1814–1878).
On the Banks of the Stream 15 × 26 in.
DR JOHN SELL COTMAN.

75b
John Joseph Cotman (1814–1878).
A River Reach 9¾ × 13¾ in.
DR JOHN SELL COTMAN.

76a
John Joseph Cotman (1814–1878).
The Flint Wall 10½ × 14¾ in.
Signed and dated: *J. J. Cotman, 1876.*
DR JOHN SELL COTMAN.

76b
Henry Jutsum (1816–1869).
Boxley, Kent 17¼ × 23 in.
Signed and dated: *Henry Jutsum*, 1850.
with THE LITTLE GALLERY, NORWICH.

77a
Henry Baines (1823–1894).
Castle Rising 7⅛ × 20⅜ in.
CASTLE MUSEUM, NORWICH.

77b
John Middleton (1827–1856).
Tonbridge 12⅝ × 18¾ in.
Signed: *Tunbridge, J. Middleton.*
CASTLE MUSEUM, NORWICH.
Ex collection: R. J. Colman.
Lit.: *Hawcroft, p. 5.*

78a
John Middleton (1827–1856).
Blofield 13 × 19 in.
Signed and dated: *Blofield, J. M. 1847.*
CASTLE MUSEUM, NORWICH.
Ex collection: R. J. Colman.

78b
John Middleton (1827–1856).
Near Butterdale, Cumberland 13 × 19 in.
Inscribed with title and date: *Sept. 1st 1846.*
MR AND MRS D. P. CLIFFORD.

79a
John Middleton (1827–1856).
Leaves 8¾ × 13½ in.
CASTLE MUSEUM, NORWICH.
Ex collection: R. J. Colman.
Lit.: *Hawcroft, p. 7.*

79b
John Middleton (1827–1856).
Study of Rocks 13 × 19 in.

CASTLE MUSEUM, NORWICH.
Ex collection: R. J. Colman.

80a
F.W. Rowland (fl. 1860).
North Quay and Town Hall, Great Yarmouth
14½ × 25⅝ in.
Signed and dated left: *W. Rowland 1860* and
inscribed centre with title.
C. H. DYER.

80b
Harry Hine (fl. 1873).
A Surrey Mill 8¼ × 12 in.
Signed and dated: *Harry Hine 1873.*
CASTLE MUSEUM, NORWICH.
Ex collection: J. W. Walker.

'The writers of Art employ the word School to denote a similarity of feeling and practice in many individuals arising from the example of one powerful mind, yet by no means implying a want of originality in the rest. In Painting, so many avenues to excellence are open, that every painter of fame is distinguished from the rest by some perfection which is to be found with himself only.'

JOHN CONSTABLE, R.A.

TO MY WIFE

Introduction

If the reputations of regional schools of painting sometimes have a faintly parochial air it is because their friends try to make out too good a case for them. It would be a pity if this were true of the Norwich School because it was never regional in a narrow sense. The School was not really isolated from the rest of England; the members of it were subject to much the same influences as their contemporaries in Bristol or Oxford, and we shall not understand them unless we relate them to other English water-colourists and see them within the general framework of the Romantic Revival.

It is not possible to say with certainty who belonged to the School and who did not, nor to say when it began and ended. The greater part of the activity which gave the School its character occurred between 1803 and 1833; but it was not evolved out of nothing and did not end suddenly, for some of its best artists did not appear until after the later date. Broadly the School extends from 1790, when Crome's apprenticeship finished, to 1878 when John Joseph Cotman died. Its nucleus is generally said to be thirty or so artists; but a School of this sort cannot be defined and the list that Dickes, for example, used for his *Norwich School of Painters*, is too short. According to a report of the Norwich Society 323 individuals had shown at its exhibitions by 1828; I have not tried to count how many more might be claimed for the School over the next fifty years. Rather than confuse the picture by trying to mention too many, I have relegated to an appendix a number of marginal artists who are bound to crop up in any consideration of the School; and as it was essentially a School of landscape I have excluded those who used water-colour for portrait or still-life only.

I have tried to show the School as a related and developing whole rather than to present the members in separate biographical studies. This may be a disadvantage for a reader who is pursuing a particular artist but I hope the gain in coherence is worth the loss in convenience. In the case of some artists the material available for study is ridiculously scant and one of the good results to be hoped for from publication is the emergence of water-colours by lesser members of the School. When this happens some of the opinions given here will no doubt have to be modified.

With a few necessary exceptions the illustrations have not been published before.

One gets tired of seeing the same picture, however important, used again and again to illustrate an artist's work as though it were the only good thing he did. When it has been necessary to refer to pictures not illustrated I have usually said where reproductions can be found.

It would have been impracticable for one who is not even an East Anglian to have undertaken this book had it not been for the generous help and advice of many who by birth or residence could claim a prescriptive right in the Norwich School. I am indebted to many private collectors who have allowed me to study and, when I wished, to illustrate their drawings; to the Right Honourable the Lord Mackintosh of Halifax, D.L., LL.D.; to Sir Edmund Bacon, Bart.; to Mr Geoffrey Allen; to Mr Alec Cotman; to Dr J. S. Cotman; to Mr Harold Day; to Mr L. G. Duke, C.B.E.; to Mr C. N. Dyer; to Mr Arnold Fellows; to Mr and Mrs Cyril Fry; to Dr L. S. Fry; to Mr E. P. Hansell; to Mr Eric Hinde; to Major Michael Ingram; to Dr and Mrs D. Kirkham; to Mr E. D. Levine; to Mr and Mrs Paul Mellon; to Mr S. Rowland Pierce, F.S.A., F.R.I.B.A.; to Mrs D. Styler; to Mr N. J. Townley; and to Dr P. A. Tyser. I am grateful to the authorities of the British, the Victoria and Albert, the National Maritime, the Fitzwilliam, and the Ashmolean Museums; to the authorities of the Tate and the Whitworth Art Galleries and of the National Gallery, Washington, and of the Museums and Art Galleries of Brighton, Bolton, Birmingham, Colchester, Doncaster, Ipswich, King's Lynn, Leeds, Luton, Maidstone, Nottingham and Sheffield. All have in various ways helped me but naturally I owe most to Dr Rajnai and to Mr Alec Cotman of the Castle Museum, Norwich, who have given me great assistance; and particularly must I say that without Mr Alec Cotman's enthusiastic help and special knowledge this book would have had little value. I must also thank the Fine Arts trade who have often aided me in my inquiries.

1

The Forerunners

THE WATER-COLOURS of the Norwich School have never collectively received the attention they deserve. This is because the popular image of the School is based on a certain type of oil-landscape created by John Crome, of which the typical subjects are large trees in full leaf, slow-moving rivers, windmills, and Norfolk cottages. The persuasive influence of these pictures gives to anything which does not comply with the specification, however well authenticated and 'of Norwich' its pedigree, something of the air of a cuckoo in the nest. Even Crome's own *Slate Quarries*, and his famous *Boulevard des Italiens*, are felt to be a betrayal of the cause. The water-colours of the School do not always treat such subjects and when they do the effect is often so different from the accepted 'Norwich School' picture that it is necessary to revise a cherished popular image: which is difficult and painful. It is this narrow view which has caused some to suggest that John Sell Cotman, who supported the Norwich Society for the greater part of its existence, who showed his pictures at its exhibitions, who presided over its deliberations and was principal drawing-master of the city for a number of years, was not *really* a Norwich School man.

Yet this neglect of the water-colour work of the School is a loss, for if we dissociate the water-colours of the Norwich artists from their oils it becomes apparent that not only was the greater body of distinctive work done in water-colour but that much of it is better than all but a few of their oil paintings.

The Norwich Society, the first public evidence of the existence of a local School of painting in the city, was formed in 1803. Its purpose was 'to conduct an Enquiry into the Rise, Progress and Present State of Painting, Architecture, and Sculpture with a view to point out the Best Methods of Study to attain to Greater Perfection in these Arts'. It is commonly supposed to have been the creation of two young professional artists of poor education, John Crome and Robert Ladbrooke, but the flavour of its manifesto smacks of the middle-class amateur. The rules were much like those of The Speculative Society,

3

which met in the same Norwich tavern 'The Hole in the Wall', and suggest that Dr Rigby, the moving spirit of the one, was behind the other. This Dr Rigby contributed something to medical science and, in the tradition of Sir Thomas Browne, was typical of the cultivated, public-spirited, professional man of the day. He occupied a central position in Norwich society and his immediate significance to us is that he was the first to employ Crome—as an errand boy. Perhaps without Dr Rigby the Norwich School would not have existed.

The fame of the Norwich School rests partly on the belief that it is the only example in England of a provincial school of painting. Yet, in England, as elsewhere, there have always been local traditions affecting the forms of the minor arts and crafts so that, for example, Wiltshire thatching is distinguishable from Norfolk thatching and Shropshire pargetting is distinct from that in Essex. On a higher level, carving in alabaster made the name of Nottingham famous throughout Europe and a certain style of manuscript illumination in the fourteenth century was so local in character that we speak of an East Anglian School of illumination. This is perhaps the far distant mainspring of our School.

Art obeys much the same laws as other forms of industry, although the laws may operate with different emphasis. An industry becomes localized because of its concern with raw materials, with markets, with communications, with operatives and their especial skills, in fact with all those things which enable it to satisfy demand. Once a skill has been established in an area it is handed down from father to son so that the continuity of the industry is ensured to the spot far *beyond* the stage when the advantages which first caused it to flourish there have decayed, and may even force it to struggle on for a little after its continuance there becomes actively disadvantageous to it. The conservatism of the medieval trade guilds only confirmed what was already inherent in the family organism with its constant awareness of the interdependence of the past, the present, and the future.[1] Art, like industry, exists to satisfy a demand, but its dependence upon the availability of raw material is less and upon traditional skills is more. Moreover the skills of the artist are not quite of the same order as those of the craftsman and industrial operative; they are more personal and his market is more ephemeral, he can more easily lose his hold on it either by idiosyncracy and inability to compromise as in Rembrandt's case, or simply by a deterioration in the quality of his creative power.

There is every reason why this should be as it is. It would be a sign of national

---

[1] Professor Pevsner has pointed out in *European Architecture* that 'Bavarian stuccoists nearly all came from the same village just as the decorators of Romanesque churches so often came from certain villages round the North Italian lakes, the makers and the vendors of plaster-of-Paris statuettes in the nineteenth century from Savoy, and the onion-men of today from Brittany'.

artistic poverty if all creative life, all vital skill, and all patronage were centred in the metropolis. The lesson of the artistic vitality of the small city states of Ancient Greece and of Renaissance Italy would seem to be that many more men have individual creative potentiality than our modern monolithic States give opportunity to. Centralization of authority combined with ease of communication leads eventually to uniformity and the disappearance of local character. By stifling provincial self-confidence a metropolis actually creates 'provincialism' and discourages the possibility of small centres of independent patronage.

The demand for works of art in Norwich in the Middle Ages arose from the number and wealth of its religious buildings. It is reckoned that there were more than 180 monastic and conventual foundations in Norfolk, and even today Norwich is bewilderingly rich in churches.[1] Upon the ornamenting of these buildings large numbers of artists were employed. The first indications of a local school are seen in the wall-paintings of Norwich churches. Professor E. W. Tristram, referring to paintings of the twelfth century, wrote: 'The workmanship was superb and of a quality unsurpassed at the period of their execution . . . they demonstrate . . . that Norwich ranked high amongst the great monastic centres of culture.[2] This was not a manifestation of the twelfth century alone for wall-painting of great accomplishment and with an East Anglian School character was done also in the early fourteenth century. As many as nineteen 'painters' lived in Norwich in the last quarter of the thirteenth century of whom all but one, Giles Le Flemming of Bruges, bore names that show they were natives of East Anglia.

It is not certain how wide was the scope of these 'painters'. They may have worked not on wall-paintings only. Of the great East Anglian Psalters it has been said, 'there is a breadth and monumental quality about the design of some of them which suggests an artist familiar with wall and panel painting'.[3] But one of the most fruitful openings for the artist was certainly glass-painting for here the destructibility of his work and the continual rebuilding of churches and enlargement of their window area led to a steady demand. Dr Woodforde gives the names of nearly sixty glass-painters who lived and worked in Norwich between 1279 and the reign of Henry VIII.[4]

The Reformation and Dissolution of the Monasteries caused a great lessening in the demand for ornamental work on religious buildings. There was still some stained glass to be

---

[1] *The Monastic Remains of Norfolk and Suffolk*, Norwich, 1934.
[2] *The Paintings of Norwich Cathedral*, Friends of the Cathedral Church of Norwich, Fifth Annual Report, 1934, II, 15.
[3] W. L. Lillie, *Proceedings of the Suffolk Inst. of Archaeol. and Nat. Hist.*, XXI, 164.
[4] *The Norwich School of Glass Painting in the Fifteenth Century*, Oxford, 1949, C. Woodforde: which contains also the references to the two preceding notes.

done in this, perhaps for colleges, guildhalls, and great houses, although this may have been little more than the representation of coats-of-arms. The demand for illuminated manuscripts failed; but by the sixteenth century a demand for portrait miniatures had arisen. By the early eighteenth century the traditional craftsmanship which had once been employed upon murals, upon the screens of churches, upon glass windows, upon the stained hangings which were the cheap substitute for tapestry, and upon the great illuminated Psalters, still persisted but was now employed chiefly on coach and sign painting, on heraldic-painting, and upon topography and portraiture.[1]

Dr Woodforde writes: 'The most marked characteristic of Norwich glass-painting in the fifteenth century is the excellence of the drawing and colouring coupled with the vigour and liveliness of the presentation of the subject matter. There is none of the courtly and faded elegance, the dreary repetitions, and the uninspired shoddiness, which is sometimes found in other parts of England. The life-stream of interest and invention was running strongly. . . . Although the style of Norwich glass-painting is unmistakably evident . . . it is not easy to define it. . . . They let white glass play a very large part in their colour schemes. . . . It is also noticeable that they avoided any suggestion of that sweetness and sentimentality which mars some contemporary work . . . there is a bracing strength and vigour which well accords with the Norfolk climate and character.' Of sixteenth-century glass he writes: 'Some of it shows a vigorous continuation of the Gothic tradition. Some shows the strong influence of continental, particularly Netherlandish art, and it is sometimes difficult to decide whether glass-painting is the work of foreigners or of Englishmen copying and adapting foreign pictures of one kind or another.' It is astonishing how much of this might have been written, *mutatis mutandis*, about the Norwich School of painters of the early nineteenth century.

The force of the local character and its power to create individual forms is shown also in monumental brasses. A. C. Bouquet writes: 'In Norfolk and Suffolk we get a great many local types of engraving, which may well proceed from a Norwich workshop, and which are totally unlike those found in other counties.'[2]

Incipient 'schools of painting' existed in other local centres as well as in Norwich. At the end of the seventeenth century a group of artists and antiquaries were centred on Francis Place in York; there was another group at Exeter about Francis Towne which included John White Abbot, Downman, John Gendall; Bristol with the Pococks, the Danbys, the Fripps, Samuel Jackson, H. Hardy, Müller, and a claim on Prout and the

---

[1] There continued to be however, some employment for glass-painters and illuminators well into the nineteenth century.
[2] *Church Brasses*, 1956. A. C. Bouquet.

Rowbothoms has a strong case; Oxford was conscious of possessing a school centred on Malchair;[1] Art Societies were formed early at Newcastle and Manchester; and Liverpool, Birmingham, and Bath all have long lists of not undistinguished local painters. The way in which many artists of the late eighteenth and early nineteenth centuries were popularly named after the towns from which they came shows that, though nationally known, they were regarded as largely living and working there—William Turner 'of Oxford', the Smiths 'of Chichester', the Barkers 'of Bath', Wright 'of Derby', Smith 'of Derby', are conspicuous but not isolated examples. Wherever a centre of population was large and prosperous enough to support a local drawing-master, a 'School' in its narrowest (though original) sense existed, so that if we could see the pictures of the pupils of Robertson 'the drunken drawing-master' hung together, a 'School of Nottingham' might emerge with a character of its own; or a shadowy 'School of Ripon' might be conjured from the work of those whom William Pearson taught.

Here, then, we have during the eighteenth and the first half of the nineteenth centuries a state of affairs which *almost* gave rise to a series of local schools. What were the favourable conditions? Why did they fail? And why did Norwich succeed? Or did it, in fact, not succeed?

To answer these questions even partially involves us in a digression. The evolution of the creative imagination that went on in England throughout the eighteenth century was neither simple nor straightforward. Men's sense of reverence and awe, deflected by Henry VIII from God to King, became, with the growth of constitutional monarchy, largely unemployed; yet the need to feel reverence and awe remained. Furthermore, man had lost confidence in his ability to create an acceptable world on his own pattern and found a new pleasure in seeing it as it was. By about 1740 also he began to feel safe enough in his social relationships to explore beyond known human boundaries into a world he had not made; and even to idealize it as the world of the Noble Savage. The concept of the Noble Savage is essentially urban as is the concept of Arcady. Roger Fry on Waley's *Introduction to the Study of Chinese Painting* commented . . . 'how, with the over-elaborate machinery of the Chinese bureaucracy . . . the desire to escape from the pressure of social life became a frequent obsession of more sensitive natures. They longed to live the life of the hermit, to live free and fearless in the isolation of the hills. It was the ideal of complete self-realization by release from social pressure. Those, too, who never even attempted this flight from society, adored mountains and torrents as symbols of escape, and for them landscape paintings, in which this aspect of nature was emphasized, became a

[1] A book by Mr Ian Fleming Williams on that most interesting group at Oxford known as 'The Great School' is to be published shortly.

source of spiritual satisfaction.'[1] This was the way in which men rediscovered the sensations of spiritual humility and it was the root cause of the Romantic Revival.

Spasmodically throughout the century the English progressed towards establishing a direct relationship with the real world about them. In painting this meant that they began to concern themselves with landscape as well as portraiture, with their surroundings as well as themselves. In a more complex way it meant that both landscape and portrait tried to come closer to the thing seen. The approach was difficult. The need to idealize was ingrained and the approach to reality was repeatedly side-tracked by the fascinating mannerisms of art.

A national school of painting in the modern sense did not exist in England until the middle of the eighteenth century. A recital of the names of the greatest artists working in England before that time reveals the truth: Holbein, Van Dyck, Peter Lely, and Godfrey Kneller were not Englishmen. Indeed it is no exaggeration to say that England did not reach her full international stature before the eighteenth century. Apart from the brilliant incident of Elizabeth I the uncertainties created by the heirs of Henry VIII had kept England from a full realization of herself until she began to mature in the reign of Anne. Then, for the first time for many centuries, she led Europe and was no longer a follower. But despite her leadership in political philosophy she was not yet fully emancipated in the field of taste. For the latter half of the seventeenth century the splendour of Louis XIV had ensured that the French version of Renaissance culture prevailed in Europe. Charles II brought with him from his exile an echo of the French Court and of French taste and stamped it upon England. The battle of Blenheim more than any other single event changed all that, but the destruction of the dominance of the French idea left—in painting at any rate—a vacuum, for there was no native tradition strong enough to fill it. Two influences now competed in England; that of the Netherlands which had never been far from us, and that of Italy which was made fashionable by the Earl of Burlington and William Kent. Nor did French influence disappear entirely; several of the few drawing-masters in England in the second quarter of the eighteenth century, men such as Gravelot and Chatelain, were French; and French influence was dominant in minor decorative painting on porcelain, enamels, and fans, for so long as the rococo was in vogue. From a synthesis of these influences, but chiefly from her own poets and from the recesses of her liberal thought, England evolved her first highly original contribution to visual art, the English garden. She also produced her first indisputably English painter, William Hogarth.

Upon these Netherlandish, Italian, and French foundations and out of these con-

[1] *The Arts of Painting and Sculpture* by Roger Fry.

flicting traditions English landscape painting at the beginning of the nineteenth century was built. From the Netherlands came realism, from Italy breadth and emotion, from France grace.

Recent research has shown that an unsuspected market for Dutch seventeenth-century landscape paintings existed in London in the early decades of the eighteenth century when at least a hundred Ruysdaels were auctioned between 1748 and 1750.[1] The original source of this demand and some at least of the supply was probably Norfolk and Suffolk. East Anglia has much in common with Holland besides commercial ties. Both are alluvial, low-lying, stoneless countries, in which land and water are in more intimate and balanced relationship than is usual elsewhere. In both countries one is conscious of spreading skies and all-pervading light. The inhabitants of both have a tradition of stubborn political and religious independence; both certainly show signs of being predisposed towards a realistic view of life; and perhaps as important as the rest, they may spring from a common stock.[2]

The Netherlands, stubbornly reformist, mercantile, incurably bourgeois, had no aristocracy of birth or taste but only of purse and there, for social and religious reasons, naturalism had sprung easily into being. The landscapes of the Ruysdaels, Van Goyen, Koninck, Hobbema, and Cuyp are the work of men who have quite a different relationship with the world about them than, for example, have Giorgione, Claude, or Salvator Rosa. At root they do not seek to use landscape for some human purpose, to establish a mood or to represent an ideal: their relationship is more humble, that of fellow creatures in a beloved creation.

The course of English painting on the road to naturalism was far from being as steady as it was in Holland. There had indeed been Netherlandish painters in the Roman tradition—such as Berchem and Jan Both, and subjective landscapists like Rembrandt; but the first were shrugged off and the second ignored: they served only to emphasize the strength and purity of the main stream. But in England there was a permanent state of contradiction: a monarchy that was not a monarchy; an aristocracy that was only half-an-aristocracy, because it did not act like one; and a reformed religion which tottered on the edge of papism. And, moreover, this dichotomy existed not only in the State but very often within the individuals who composed the State, for few were all Tory or all Whig—so that every man being true to half-himself was being false to half-himself. Here, for example, is Gainsborough wishing 'to take my Viol de Gamba and walk off to some sweet

[1] Apollo: November 1962—John Hayes, *Gainsborough's Early Landscapes.*
[2] Between 1565 and 1569, 3,000 refugees from Alva's persecution in the Netherlands settled in Norwich. *History Today*: January 1964, *The Duke in his Country*: Neville Williams.

village where I can paint landskips' but failing to drag himself away from London and Bath and fashionable portraits when he could perfectly well have done so. Here is the source of the strange contradiction in their garden-landscaping which, despite all protestations that it sought to imitate Nature, only reproduced on the one hand the mannered poetic landscapes of the Roman breed, and on the other, evolved the ideal landscape of Lancelot Brown—but left Nature as far away as ever. Both Wilson and Gainsborough pushed out in the direction of the natural vision, but Wilson nearly starved and Gainsborough turned back. The contrived landscapes of de Loutherbourg and Zuccarelli gave an easier and more quickly comprehended pleasure.

This, then, was the condition of the art-loving world of England when the Norwich School of painters began to take shape in the 1790s. It was not only the state of mind of those who were to paint the pictures which mattered, but the state of mind of those who talked about pictures, who admired and bought them, for it is to a great extent the nature of the patronage which establishes the peculiar quality of a School. The French wars had stimulated national patriotism to the point that connoisseurs were prepared to believe that amongst *English* painters painting *English* scenery great art might be found.[1] Patriotism can easily become a contracting rather than an expanding loyalty and if the upper classes were prepared to think well of English painters because they were English the middle classes of Norwich were prepared to think well of Norwich painters simply because they were of Norwich. Sir Martin Shee, who later became P.R.A., even wrote a poem justifying such an attitude, arguing that pictures should be bought from 'heart' (i.e. motives of loyalty) rather than 'taste'; and the Norwich Society placed the quotation at the head of one of their exhibition catalogues.

It has been said that the prosperity of Norwich was one cause of the growth of its school of artists but, in fact, the city did not share in the general prosperity of England. Whereas other cities experienced the population explosion which accompanied the Industrial Revolution the numbers of Norwich did not increase proportionately.[2] Stagnation may actually have created more favourable conditions because the Norwich merchants, unlike the newly-rich industrialists of Manchester and Liverpool, had been thrown up by

[1] Although it gained greatly in force towards the end of the century this was not a new idea. Francis Haskell in *Patrons and Painters*, 1963, quotes Alesandro Galilei, a Flemish architect who arrived in England in 1714: 'the English do not behave like people in Italy, where a foreigner arrives with a barest hint of talent, everyone rushes after him and native artists with far greater abilities are left behind. Here it is just the opposite because they want to employ their own countrymen though they are complete donkeys.'

[2] Between 1801 and 1831 Liverpool moved from 82,000 to 202,000; Manchester from 95,000 to 238,000; and Sheffield and Birmingham both doubled their populations. Norwich, on the other hand, went from 37,000 to 50,000 only.

an earlier wave of prosperity and were at least of the third generation. This meant that they were a class by themselves, educated, responsible, and with some leisure, clear now of the mêlée at the foot of Fortune's ladder but not yet forgetful that its base was on the ground. Unlike the old landed gentry they were still in touch with the city because their financial roots were still there, and again unlike them, they were men whose taste had not been Italianized by the Grand Tour and its inherited souvenirs.

The most notable of the Norwich patrons was Harvey of Catton. Catton House was outside the walls but not more than a mile or so from the city centre. Thomas Harvey, a master weaver and merchant banker, was an amateur artist and collector of pictures. He is known to have had Gainsborough's *Cottage Door*, Wilson's *View on the Coast of Baiae*, Jan Steen's *The Christening Feast*, Tintoretto's *Embarkation of St Ursula* and landscapes by Salvator Rosa, Gaspard Poussin, Cuyp, and Hobbema. Other important local collectors were John Patterson, Dawson Turner, the banker of Yarmouth, and the Beauchamps of Langley Hall. But collectors were not the only patrons to influence taste. The greater part of an artist's income came from teaching and the opinions of those who employed the drawing-masters inevitably affected their practice. Often the industrialists and merchants of East Anglia were men of dissenting stock who had been impelled to trade by the disabilities imposed on them for their religious views. Towards the end of the eighteenth century many things led to a relaxation of practice amongst the more puritanical Non-comformist sects, and families such as the Gurneys, although Quakers, no longer set themselves against such pursuits as drawing, music, or on occasion, even dancing. But their approach to drawing lessons needed a moral justification. Mrs John Gurney of Earlham drew up rules for the education of her children which she begins 'As it appears to be our reasonable duty to improve our faculties, and by that means to render ourselves useful . . .' and then commends the study of English, Latin, French, 'the simple beauties of mathematics', ancient and modern history, geography, chronology, . . . 'to these may be added a knowledge of the most approved branches of natural history, *and a capacity for drawing from nature,* in order to promote that knowledge and facilitate the pursuit of it'. It is not surprising that the teacher, John Crome, selected for such drawing should prove to be a realist rather than a mannerist.

The taste of the time had already to a great extent explored that rough, masculine, and dramatic quality in scenery known as the 'picturesque'. By the 1780s it had been sufficiently publicized by its chief theorist, William Gilpin (1724–1804), in his series of *Picturesque Tours* for it to have become the current vogue for persons of taste. It was sought for everywhere but chiefly in rugged mountain districts such as Wales, Scotland, and the Lake District. Between 1750 and 1795 sixty books were published on the Alps, and artists such as Towne and Cozens came back to England with their sketchbooks full of precipices and torrents. Others, like Pars, sought that aspect of the picturesque which was to be found in the classical ruins of the Mediterranean, although there the pure cult of the picturesque was adulterated by archaeological and topographical motives. The taste for the exotic, a specialized aspect of the picturesque symptomatic of the European's widening horizons, sent William Hodges, the Daniells, William Alexander, and Thomas Hearne in search of material to the South Seas, to India, China, and the West Indies. The 'picturesque' as an artistic attitude of mind was susceptible of development in two ways: it could concentrate on its subjective aspect and become intensely imaginative, almost expressionist; or it could refine upon the human experience in the face of nature and distil subtle emotion from the most reticent of subjects. To the merchants of Norwich and Yarmouth whose wealth had been acquired in traditional ways in the eighteenth century and upon whose walls hung Ruysdaels, Cuyps, and Hobbemas, to whom 'truth' was more important than display, and between whom and London lay 100 miles of bad roads, the second of these alternatives appealed. Fortunately for the art of the English Landscape the wars with France caused difficulties of foreign travel which limited supplies of the exotic for over twenty years, so that artists who might otherwise have looked beyond England were forced to look more closely at her.

The process of seeing the ordinary English landscape with delight had already begun with Wilson and Gainsborough but it made little general progress until the 1790s. Nor was the development of this theme even then the peculiar property of the Norwich School, nor of East Anglia, though its greatest exponents—Gainsborough, Constable, and Crome—all came from there. Constable's saying 'there is room enough for a natural painter' was echoed in many parts of England and might have been said, for example, by David Cox or Peter de Wint. But it certainly must have been said more whole-heartedly in Norwich than elsewhere.

Amongst this somewhat isolated society there were in the last quarter of the eighteenth century a number of painters of a modest sort who were Norwich men. There was John Ninham (1754–1817) who seems to have been chiefly an engraver and heraldic-painter, although he may also have been a topographical draughtsman in the stained drawing tradition. Very little survives that can be attributed to him with confidence. There is a monochrome drawing in Norwich Castle of *Norwich from the South-East* (Cot. and Haw., page 14, Plate 5) (Plate 1a) and also a series of drawings made in 1792–3 which were published in a book *Views of the Gates of Norwich* in 1861 (Cot. and Haw., page 118, Plate 11). These show him to have been a topographer in the tradition of Wenceslaus Hollar.

Of James Sillett (1764–1840) we know more. He eventually became President of the Norwich Society and a good deal of his work survives. He, like Ninham, had been brought up to the trade of heraldic painting but left Norwich and was a pupil at the Royal Academy from 1781 to 1790. He exhibited at the Academy in 1796 and for the next forty-one years contributed his speciality of meticulously painted still-life, fruit, and flower studies, varied with occasional miniatures. For much of his life he was a drawing-master at King's Lynn, and consequently was only an Honorary Member of the Norwich Society until he came to live in the city in 1811. He was also a frequent topographer and published a book of Norwich churches in 1828. Several of his topographical monochromes are in Norwich Castle (Cotman and Hawcroft illustrate eight of them) and although the drawing is by no means faultless they have a pleasantly sensitive simplicity which is somehow missed in reproduction. His fruit and flower studies, of which there are several at Norwich and more in the British Museum, are good of their sort; their sort being water-colour versions of Van Huysum (Plate 4a). The only landscape by him which shows something of the same delicacy of touch as his flower-paintings is *The Old Oak at Winfarthing* (Plate 4b) in which he has handled the tree as though it were a flower. Sillett, a true professional painter who could turn his hand to anything, maintained himself while he was in London partly by scene-painting, to which he was helped by another Norwich man, William Capon.

Capon (1757–1827) was the son of an artist, though whether the father was also a Norwich man is not known. He began as a portrait painter, went to London, worked on the decorations for Ranelagh Gardens and the Italian Opera House, became scene-painter at Drury Lane and settled down as an architectural draughtsman. In the Crace Collection at the British Museum there is a fresh little water-colour of *The Opera House in the Haymarket* in quite strong colour (Plate 2b). He seems to have done a number of these beautifully finished frontal elevations of town buildings. Other drawings by him are in the London Museum. Although he is said to have left Norwich early in his career and, unlike Sillett, not to have returned to settle in his native city, he exhibited at the Norwich Society as late as 1823 when he was described as 'Draughtsman and Painter of Architecture and Landscape to H.R.H. the Duke of York'. There are five entries under that date which from their description seem not to have been such starkly topographical subjects as his early work, although he was still clearly a topographer. Two of these drawings were in 'Italian Chalk'.

Earlier than any of these was Charles Catton (1728–98), born at Norwich but apprenticed to a coach-painter in London. It is said that he was the first heraldic-painter to design the supporters to coats-of-arms naturalistically which, if true, was probably responsible for his appointment as coach-painter to George III. The King nominated him one of the founder-members of the Royal Academy (1768). His exhibits at the Academy were chiefly landscapes, with occasional animal pictures and compositions. In the Victoria and Albert there is a fine *View of the Bridges at Hawick* attributed to Catton (Plate 1b), and Cotman and Hawcroft illustrate an engraving after a painting by him (page 54, Plate 24, *Cathedral from the North-East*). There are also engravings after him in the British Museum, memorably one of *Love* (as a little child) *taming Rage* (a lion), in which the lion is rendered with angry realism and the child with a saccharinal quality associated more with the nineteenth than the eighteenth century.

His son, also Charles Catton, trained under his father and at the Royal Academy Schools. He exhibited at the Royal Academy from 1776–1800. He was a painter of theatrical scenery, an illustrator, an animal draughtsman and a topographer. His water-colour, *A View of Norwich from Mousehold Hill, near the ruins of Ketts Castle*, is in the Victoria and Albert Museum (Plate 2a). It was probably done shortly before it was engraved in 1792 and has the charm of its date and its kind. Three fine imperial architectural water-colours of abbey ruins attributed to him are in the Ashmolean; they seem distinctly related to Charles Catton senior's *Bridge at Hawick* and either father or son may have done all four. They are firm, sensitive in line and colour, and as good as anything that was done in that vein. The British Museum has a series of large coloured engravings after the son by F. Jukes; they are of broadly-seen landscapes of the Scottish border, topographical in interest with castles and ruins and mansions but always containing a lively human interest in the manner of Michael Angelo Rooker. There are also engravings by the son after Morland. He became wealthy and emigrated to America in 1804 so that he need concern us no more.

More interesting than these is William Williams, known as Williams 'of Norwich' to distinguish him from all the others, to whom the Society of Arts awarded a premium in 1758 and who exhibited at the Royal Academy between 1770 and 1792. I know of only two undoubted water-colours by him, one in Norwich Castle and one in the Victoria and Albert. Both are signed and dated 1795 and treat of a similar subject—vagrants with a donkey in a wooded landscape—in a similar manner (Plates 3a and 3b). These are good water-colours which show a distinct relationship to the work of Thomas Barker of Bath and, perhaps, of George Morland, but they are more 'themselves' than anybody else though they are of the lineage of Berchem. On the evidence of these two pictures alone Williams appears as an original artist, but where is the remainder of his work and what is it like? The portfolios of Stark's drawings in the Colman Collection at Norwich contain a water-colour which treats of a similar donkey and attendants; it is unsigned, and has a number of points of difference, but it also may be by Williams.

Other forerunners of the Norwich School were Joseph Brown (1720–1801), known as 'the Norwich Claude', Edward Miles and William Stevenson who were both miniature-painters, Thomas Holloway (1748–1847), and Thomas Bardwell (1704–67). Mention of these men, whose work has for the most part disappeared from view and whose names are known now only to students of the by-ways of art, serves to show that there was a local tradition of painting which led back through the heraldic-painters as far perhaps as to the twelfth century, and that there were local examples that a journeyman coach-and-sign painter could graduate to higher forms of art.

This tradition may not have been without its effect upon John Crome (1768–1821) who, after a few months as Dr Rigby's errand boy, was apprenticed to Francis Whisler, a coach-painter.

Crome, the son of a journeyman weaver and ale-house keeper, was fourteen years older than Cotman, ten years older than Varley, eight years older than Constable, seven years older than Turner and Girtin. He was born in the year in which the Royal Academy was founded, with Sir Joshua Reynolds as President and among its founder-members Gainsborough, Richard Wilson, Paul Sandby, and Charles Catton of Norwich. By birth he was almost of an earlier generation than the vintage years of the English water-colour school but he was a slow developer. His apprenticeship ended in 1790—by then he was 22; at 23 Turner had exhibited at the Royal Academy and at 27 had been elected an R.A.; Girtin at 21 had exhibited at the Academy and at 27 was dead—his life's work done; Cotman and Varley were both well-known among connoisseurs by the time they were 22; but of Crome at a like age all we know with certainty is that he had ended his apprenticeship as a coach-painter and sign-writer and become for a few months a journeyman painter in the employment of his master.

Crome as a water-colourist has been a shadowy figure. Amongst the drawings attributed to him there appear to be several hands, and the evidence for even the few undisputed works is slighter than one would wish. Even in 1838 Dawson Turner referred to his water-colours as comparatively rare and now he is amongst the rarest of the masters.

Few great artists are more reticent and anonymous than Crome. There is an essential modesty about the man, a suppression of personality, an avoidance of mannerism, which means that his work, if stamped at all, is stamped in a negative sense—'Crome would never have done this', 'Crome would have eliminated that'. It has been said that he rarely, if ever, signed; this is not true although there is no doubt that some of the signatures purporting to be his are not. From 1805 until his death in 1821 his contribution to the Norwich Society Exhibitions is catalogued, but often there is no distinction made between paintings and drawings, no measurements are given, and subjects are frequently repeated and usually inadequately described. Of his 286 exhibits thirteen can be securely identified as oil-sketches, seventeen as drawings—perhaps in pencil, perhaps in monochrome wash, perhaps in water-colour—and the remaining 256 may be in any medium although most were probably in oil.

Crome is not part of the central tradition of English water-colour if one accepts it as running from the early topographers through Dayes to Turner and Girtin. He belongs rather to that other line of development which is represented by Dürer, Ostade, Van Dyck, Taverner, Gainsborough, the Gilpins, and Monro, a tradition which is founded on the water-colour sketch considered essentially as no more than a private indulgence by a painter in oils. He was not therefore particularly sensitive to the change of vision and technique which became fairly general in the period 1798–1805, and we cannot necessarily date his drawings in relation to this water-shed period.

When his apprenticeship to the coach-painter ended in 1790 Crome was already associated with Robert Ladbrooke (1768–1842) and shared with him an attic studio. Ladbrooke was apprenticed to White, a printer who was also an amateur artist. Together Crome and Ladbrooke copied prints and may have hand-coloured them for sale as other young artists were doing in London. In effect they constituted themselves an 'academy' and taught themselves drawing by methods not unlike those of Dr Monro's famous evening gatherings in London. Probably it was before his apprenticeship ended that Crome made the acquaintance of Thomas Harvey of Catton and became a regular visitor to Harvey's collection of pictures. Harvey was himself an amateur artist and Crome perhaps watched him at work. According to Iolo Williams, who had seen some of Harvey's drawings, they were rather in the manner of George Frost of Ipswich, thus confirming the relationship with Gainsborough which one would expect.

After his apprenticeship ended Crome set up on his own. From 1790 until 1803 when the Norwich Society was started he seems to have scratched a living as an odd-job artist about the city, painting inn-signs (of which two survive) and taking on anything that offered. He also set up as a drawing-master and gradually gained so considerable a reputation in this line of business, no doubt with the help of Dr Rigby and Thomas Harvey, that by 1798 he was drawing-master to the daughters of one of the most influential families of the county, the Gurneys of Earlham.

At one time it was uncritically accepted that the Norwich School was the spontaneous creation of John Crome alone and that he, an untutored genius, evolved a school of landscape painting which owed nothing to any previous painter except Hobbema; in effect that he used his eyes on the local Norfolk country-side and painted what he saw. But Crome was self-taught only in the sense that he underwent no regular pupillage save as a

Plate I *The Mill Wheel* John Crome (1768–1821)

coach-painter. This does not mean he did not pick up lessons and absorb influences where he could. From his apprenticeship we should expect him first to have learned a proper understanding and appreciation of his materials; secondly, from the sign-painting side of the trade, a capacity to conceive a picture in broad terms of light and dark; and thirdly from heraldic-painting, gilding, and lettering, an ability to do fine accurate work in detail.

Whisler the coach-painter was his technical master, but the masters of his spirit were Wilson, Gainsborough, perhaps Barker of Bath, Hobbema, Ruysdael, and Van der Neer, those whose work he was able to study at Catton and whom Harvey would naturally encourage him to emulate. Of these the earliest influences, so one judges from his oils, were Wilson, Gainsborough, and Barker; his love for Hobbema came later.

The typical Norwich landscape which Crome created during these uncharted years avoids on the one hand the prosaically topographical, although by far the greater part of it represents recognized places; and, on the other hand, it rejects the imaginative and subjective approach to landscape, although its best work is always the product of intense personal feeling.

The difference between the topography of Crome and the traditional topographical draughtsman is the difference between a poem and an architect's bill of quantities. Crome chose his subjects because of the pictures he could make from them, not because of their intrinsic interest as ancient monuments or architectural examples. Nor, when he set himself to paint a windmill or a wherry, did he create an imagined turbulence of spirit in the way that Turner did in order to give false drama to his subject. Nor, having rejected the appeal to the mind and the appeal of obvious emotion, did he take the third easy path to popular esteem of elegant, mannered, or brilliantly dexterous execution. In this respect as in all others he was the reverse of Turner. In his often quoted letter to Stark in which he urged breadth and unity Crome wrote—'trifles in nature must be overlooked that we may have our feelings raised by seeing the whole picture at a glance, not knowing how or why we are so charmed'.

Crome must have done a fair body of work before the Society was formed, for it was the underlying vision of landscape as he taught it to his fellow-townsmen which gave the Norwich School at first such homogeneity as it had. It was his peculiar triumph that he should have made this vision acceptable, for it is not obvious in its appeal, and its charms, I suspect, require aesthetic sensibility combined with a sort of innocent directness of vision if they are to be appreciated. These are not common qualities.

2

The Norwich Society:
First Period 1803-12

IN 1803 the Norwich Society was founded, according to tradition on the initiative of Crome and Ladbrooke, and perhaps at first conceived as an extension of their shared studio arrangement. There is no list of its original membership. The first exhibition was held in 1805. Crome showed twenty-two pictures, Robert Ladbrooke fourteen, Charles Hodgson fourteen, Robert Dixon sixteen, and John Thirtle five. These are all men who became recognized later as leading members of the School; others who exhibited were W. C. Leeds, A. Browne, E. Bell, Mrs Coppin, J. Freeman, Miss Freeman, Mrs Frewer, Mr Gibson, The Rev. W. Gordon, W. Harwin, Miss Jacobs, Master Leeds, J. Percy, F. Stone, J. Blake, and a Mr Crotch—a relative of the now much-loved Dr Crotch. Among the contributions of the lesser figures were architectural plans and elevations, copies after Barker of Bath, and probably some engravings and pieces of sculpture.

Of Crome's contributions some were mere sketches and many were probably in water-colour. Most of his known water-colours give the impression of being of this period and if later he almost forsook water-colour we easily explain Dawson Turner's statement that his water-colours were rare.

The known events of Crome's relatively uneventful life give rather less help in dating his early drawings than one might expect. In 1792 he married; by 1798 he had so far established himself as to be drawing-master to the Gurneys of Earlham; in 1802 he went with the Gurneys on their summer tour in the Peak and Lake Districts; in 1803 he went, perhaps with Robert Ladbrooke, perhaps again with the Gurneys, to South Wales, for by the date of the first Norwich Society Exhibition he had visited the Wye and Severn country, seeing Goodrich, Chepstow, Tintern, and Piercefield. Although the Gurney diaries record their trip to South Wales in 1803 Crome is not mentioned in the published portions for that year.

Like other artists Crome based work on his own sketches years after they were done, so that subject is not necessarily an indication of date. It is safe to say that Crome, except when frankly copying, rarely painted what he had not seen; but he may have seen it long before he painted it. Cumberland recurs as a subject in the list of his exhibited works quite frequently from 1805 to 1817 but he is thought to have been there on two occasions only, in 1803 and 1811. Likewise with the Wye subjects: a visit which is thought to have taken place in 1803 gave rise to pictures exhibited in 1805, 1806, 1807, and 1809. Nevertheless there probably were other trips both to the north and to the west of which we know nothing.

Among Crome's earliest surviving water-colours is *The Mill Wheel* (Colour Plate I) The drawing was first made in grey monochrome and the colour added afterwards, a well-known eighteenth-century technique which suggests a date perhaps as early as 1795. Already the breadth of conception and the great calm which pervades this drawing show fully developed that essential quality of Crome which Iolo Williams called 'a robust and yet gracious nobility and simplicity of mind'; no other full water-colours in this early manner are known although some probably still exist. The next in date are likely to be those which show clear signs that Crome had seen the work of Girtin. It is not difficult to see Girtin's influence in nearly all the later water-colours of Crome but in some it is so strong that we can safely assume that it was still fresh. The impressive grey-brown monochrome *Whitlingham* (Iolo Williams, Plate CXXII) and *Near Lakenham* (Plate 6a) both in the Castle Museum, Norwich, are not far from Girtin of 1800.

It is not certain what time-lag we should allow for influences from London to reach Norwich; perhaps very little. If so we must attribute to 1801 those few almost 'blue' drawings which Crome probably did in response to the stimulus of Cotman's much more emphatic 'blues' of that year. The two best of these are *By the Roadside* (Plate 7b) in the Whitworth and *Mountainous Landscape* (Plate 8a) in the collection of Mr L. G. Duke. These two drawings in turn connect with a number of others: the Whitworth picture with *Trees on a Bank* (Plate 8b) at the British Museum, and with Sir Edmund Bacon's *The River through the Trees* (Plate 9a), as well as with others: and Mr Duke's picture with *The Sunken Lane* (Plate 9b) at the British Museum, with *Mountain Scene* in the same collection, and, notably, with *Patterdale* (Plate 6b), a splendid monochrome in the Fitz-william Museum. The last, if it is correctly identified, was shown at Norwich in 1805 but was certainly done some years before. These mountain scenes may be from the 1802 tour with the Gurneys to the Peak and Lake Districts but are more likely to be from an earlier unrecorded tour in 1800. *The Mill Wheel* which at first sight appears not to be an East Anglian subject and suggests an earlier journey still is, in fact, probably one of the water-mills in the neighbourhood of King's Lynn.

Of the Wye Valley subjects three water-colours of Tintern are at Norwich Castle. The two from the Colman Collection are probably those exhibited in 1805 (Plate 7a); the third which has recently been acquired by the Norwich Museum may be the one exhibited in 1807; it is the finest but is not necessarily, on that account, later. One other important drawing, *The Demolition of the Cathedral Infirmary* (Cot. and Haw., page 49, Plate 18) at Norwich Castle, can also be given to 1805 as the infirmary was demolished in that year.

On grounds of apparent indebtedness to Gainsborough we might be inclined to give an early date to *The Blacksmith's Shop at Hingham* (Plate 10b) in the Doncaster Art Gallery; but such arguments, unless supported by an early technique, are not to be relied on, for Crome exhibited similar subjects in 1807, 1808, and 1811. Although these may not have been Gainsboroughesque his *Sketch in the style of Gainsborough* exhibited in 1806 shows that this early influence may be found later in Crome's work than we would expect.

To a rather later date I should ascribe several major pictures: the *Grove Scene* in the collection of Mr E. P. Hansell; the *Entrance to Earlham Park* now in the Mellon Collection (Plate 10a): *The Glade Cottage* in the collection of Lord Mackintosh (Plate 11b); the *Wood Scene* in the Victoria and Albert (Plate 12), and the version of the same picture in Norwich Castle.

Few full water-colours attributed convincingly to Crome differ in essential style from these which we can place between 1800 and 1807. Technically as a water-colourist he was not advanced and he made small use of those devices which, first tentatively employed in the last quarter of the eighteenth century, were fully exploited by Turner and the artists who derive from him. It has been well said that although water-colour had long been used in England and on the Continent for various purposes, water-colour as it began to be used at the end of the eighteenth century was a distinct art form. In the sense that this is true Crome seems to be not of the English water-colour school at all. He used water-colour rather as Dürer and Van Dyck[1] used it and not because he saw in a water-colour way. Although he is credited with having introduced the trick of 'graining' in house-painting, Crome strikes one as a man very little interested in techniques, one who was very unlikely to be over-fascinated by the means because the end was so clearly before his eyes. But, though Crome made little use of scratching and stippling and stopping, and employed

[1] Would it be safer to say 'the Master of the water-colour landscapes formerly attributed to Van Dyck'?

a limited palette, the originality of his vision is evident. There is scarcely a trace in his mature work of the Italianism of Wilson whom he had so much admired and copied, nor of the mannered Frenchness of Gainsborough to whom almost equally he had been indebted. The 'picturesque' also is almost entirely absent and has taken with it the sense of 'picture-making'. There are many drawings which show that he was affected by the all-pervading influence of Girtin; there are others which may show Cotman's influence, but in neither case do the superficialities remain: if he learned from them it was in the way of vision and not of tricks. All his work has the air of being a direct and honest record of a thing seen, a simplicity which throughout his life is a hall-mark of Crome's work in both mediums. It is not to be supposed that this artlessness was achieved unselfconsciously or without the employment of a high degree of art; we know that it was not. To attain it he avoided everything in the nature of 'picture-making'—in the words of his famous letter to James Stark—'that we may have our feelings raised . . . not knowing how or why we are so charmed'.[1] The result is often that a Crome at first sight seems clumsily constructed, that his space looks overfilled because he has avoided using the proportions, repoussoirs, and traditional methods of the picture constructor.[2]

His colour, rarely strong, is often rather faded and sometimes, as in *Trees by Water* (Plate 14b), changed to a bright russet. Of later pictures the Whitworth's *Houses and Wherries on the Wensum* (Plate 13) and Norwich Castle's *Silver Birches; after Pynacker* (Plate 14a) are still strong. Colour for its own sake did not fascinate Crome as it did so many of his contemporaries, nor did he normally seek to record those extravagant effects of nature which involve an extreme palette and which most water-colourists of the nineteenth century pursued pertinaciously but with varying success. Atmosphere he sought and obtained; storms, rainbows, and apocalyptic sunsets he left to others. To say that his colour is slight is not to say that it is poor. Where it has survived it is clear, true, and harmonious, but like all else in Crome's work it is reticent and subservient to the whole.

That he was not over-impressed by the function of colour is implied by the considerable body of monochrome wash drawing by him. Sometimes carried out with brush alone and sometimes with brush and pencil, these delicate grey wash drawings contain at times almost more of the essential genius of Crome than his full water-colours and his oils. Their combination of strength and fragility makes them seem like delicate fragments from an early Chinese scroll painting. I do not recollect that it has been remarked before

[1] *See* Appendix D.
[2] This appearance is often accentuated by the modern tendency to hang pictures too low. Crome's work should nearly always be seen at, or slightly above, eye-level: as indeed should almost everybody's.

but I believe that the English practice of making monochrome wash drawings is broadly confined between 1790 and 1810 and that, although many exceptions will readily come to mind, by far the majority of dateable examples would fall within that period—and those in grey rather than blue in the latter half of it. In Crome's case this dating is supported by some of the subjects and by the similarity of handling in them all.[1]

He was often poor at figures as were most of the Norwich School and, indeed, nearly all landscapists of the period except Constable and Joshua Cristall. Crome's figures are usually neckless and are often in ungainly attitudes. Perhaps the capacity to simplify which is essential for landscape painters is responsible for reducing their figures to posturing sugar-bags. When present the figures in Crome's work usually take a natural place, although in the two earlier Tintern drawings one recalls the ubiquitous gesturing travellers of the Gilpins, and the recurrent banditti of Salvator Rosa. But this sort of 'picturesque furnishing figure' is really quite remote from Crome's work.

Of the other leading exhibitors of the first exhibition we have already mentioned Robert Ladbrooke (1770–1842) as the apprentice with whom Crome shared a studio. The studio arrangement probably lasted until 1792 when Crome married Phoebe Berney, but the association did not then end for in 1793 Ladbrooke married Phoebe's sister; thus in the second generation we have John Berney Crome and John Berney Ladbrooke.

Ladbrooke, although he is said to have been a co-founder of the Norwich Society, has been overshadowed and almost obliterated by Crome. Crome was a well-liked companionable person; Ladbrooke was not. Crome has been the subject of essays, biographies, memoirs, and monographs; Ladbrooke of a few paragraphs. So Ladbrooke, a phantasmal personality of whom few authentic works are known, has suffered the fate of all such ill-defined figures by becoming a rubbish bin for a multitude of unidentified works or, alternatively, of being denied any works at all. In their apprentice days it is said that Crome monopolized the landscape work and that Ladbrooke did the portraits, for which he received 5*s* a time. Like Crome he was probably an oil painter by preference and his watercolours are rare. To the exhibition of 1805 Ladbrooke sent thirteen pictures. One of these is described as *A Set Piece; body colour*; one was an oil that he had exhibited previously at the Royal Academy; and, of the remainder, six derive from a trip to Wales during which he seems to have visited Llangollen, Conway, Llanrwst, Chepstow, and Tintern. This looks like two separate journeys, of which that to South Wales was probably made with Crome.

---

[1] Messrs Sotheby on 20 November 1963 sold a pencil and blue and grey wash drawing inscribed 'Drawn in 1800 part blown down, pulled down in September and January 1802' which, although the inscription is not in Crome's hand, may well be true. It is now in the collection of Mr and Mrs Paul Mellon.

In the British Museum there are two water-colours which were in the Reeve Collection, *Near Carrow Bridge* (Iolo Williams, Plate CXX), and *On the Coast* (Dickes, page 178). These probably represent work from different periods. The first combines strength and delicacy in a way one associates with Crome and probably dates from their close friendship. The second retains the breadth but the strength has coarsened; the lessons Crome taught have not been forgotten but have become a formula. In Norwich Castle there is a monochrome of *Sandling Ferry* (Cot. and Haw., page 20, Plate 16) which was lithographed in 1806 and can safely be attributed to that or the preceding year; but the major work at Norwich is a large upright of a bridge over a mountain stream, rather heavily painted in dark rich colours, *Glymllffes Bridge, North Wales* (Plate 17a), which is inscribed by James Reeve[1] as having been bought at J. B. Ladbrooke's sale. The subject of the picture, its form, and its technical approach, are reminiscent of Crome but it lacks Crome's passages of delicate strength and his atmospheric perception, as well as being altogether darker and richer in tone than any Crome drawing we know. The brushwork, which is like that of *Near Carrow Bridge*, confirms the latter's early date, probably 1803, the date of Ladbrooke's Welsh tour. Another picture undoubtedly by the same hand and in a similarly dark palette is in Mr and Mrs Cyril Fry's collection (Plate 15b).

Apart from these there are four in my own collection which are, I believe, by Robert Ladbrooke. The earliest, *The Waggoner and Oak* (Plate 15a), is a large drawing in black wash heightened with white on blue paper; it is similar in brushwork to the Welsh bridge and has the full flavour of an early Norwich School picture. Also on blue paper but of a later date are two simple wash drawings in brown and black of coastal scenes, probably Cromer, which came from Sir George Hayter's collection; these relate to the British Museum's *On the Coast*. The last is a moonlit evening scene in full water-colour of a wayside forge with Norwich in the distance (Plate 16). Judging from the broad washes this is late and there is little of Crome's influence now apparent, but the darkness of tone characteristic of the Welsh bridge picture is still there. Ladbrooke's son, John Berney Ladbrooke (of whom more later) showed *Blacksmith's Shop—Moonlight* at Norwich in 1848 but I do not think this can be his work, although he may well have based a painting upon his father's drawing. Two lithographs by Robert Ladbrooke, dated 1806, are illustrated by Cotman and Hawcroft (page 30, Plates 2 and 3).

From consideration of all this material a distinct impression of Ladbrooke's artistic personality builds up. There is much in him that is like Crome, but his brushwork though generally free and flashing is less subtle, his later washes are more broad, and the general

[1] Appendix B.

effect left by his pictures is rather saturnine and gloomy, as though they are the work of a temperamental solitary.

Next in importance of the exhibitors of 1805 was John Thirtle (1777–1839), the son of a cobbler. As a boy he worked at a frame-makers in London and when qualified returned to Norwich to open a shop where he dealt in frames and pictures, and sold miniatures painted by himself. Some Norwich School pictures are still to be found in their original Thirtle frames.

Thirtle is an original and distinctive artist who succeeded in receiving influences from Crome and from Cotman without losing his individuality. He may have known Cotman before the latter went to London in 1798; he is said to have sought out Cotman's drawings at Ackerman's shop in the Strand and eventually he married the sister of Cotman's wife as Ladbrooke had Crome's. But though, as we shall see when we discuss Cotman's work, some later Thirtles show his influence they could never be mistaken for Cotmans, whereas there has been and still is occasional confusion between the work of Thirtle and Crome, particularly in their grey wash drawings.

The earliest recorded Thirtle is *A Windmill* which was catalogued in 1886 by the Norwich Art Circle as having been done in 1800. It was a landscape, but his contribution to the 1805 exhibition did not show him primarily as a landscapist for it consisted of two portraits, a copy of a classical subject after Westall, and two drawings, *Cottages* and *Welsh Cottages*. Dickes assumes that these portraits and those exhibited in the following year were miniatures but they were probably semi-miniatures of the scale we associate with Downman. But though there were in his contribution to the second exhibition, six portraits, two imaginative subjects—*A Nymph Bathing* and *Despairing Lover*, and one interior, there were now also eight landscapes which suggests that he was beginning to find landscape more congenial or more lucrative.

As a portraitist and a subject painter Thirtle was no better and no worse than many competent artists who at that time worked the same field (Plate 17b). By some trick of mind those who could look at a tree or a building without sentimentalizing it no sooner attempted the human figure than a fearful posturing self-consciousness seized them by the throat and choked all visual sincerity out of them. In landscape it is quite another matter and Thirtle stands high as a minor master in a period that was very fruitful of them. He did not go to the same lengths as Crome in an effort to give the impression of an unaffected, unselected chunk of nature; one is aware that his subjects are organized on the paper in a well-proportioned harmonious way, but there is little that is forced, self-conscious, or 'picturesque' about it. His subjects, such scenes as river-reaches in the evening light, are in themselves not remarkable and he rarely tried to make them

Plate II *Timber Yard and Norwich Cathedral from the North* John Thirtle (1777–1839)

so; nor does he seem to have travelled in search of sketching grounds, for with the exception of some London drawings all the Thirtles known to me are of East Anglia.

Technically Thirtle is a pure water-colourist who rarely seeks to emulate the effects of oil and has a loving understanding of his medium. Of all the Norwich men he is nearest to Peter de Wint (Plates 18a, 18b, 19a). Unfortunately he theorized on chromatics and evolved a warm and attractive grey which he nearly always used. As they were well-liked his pictures were hung, and the blue component of the grey having flown in the light the majority of Thirtles are ruddy shadows of their former selves. This characteristic is so marked that there is a tendency for all pictures so disfigured to be labelled as Thirtles, although they are clearly by his pupils and imitators. Conversely, it has become difficult to accept as Thirtles those drawings which do not contain this treacherous grey (Plate 19b). His handling is generally free and soft and often gives the impression that he washed or dabbed his drawings with a sponge so that they have an appearance of granulation, though not so obviously as G. Fennell Robson's.

Robert Dixon (1780–1815), the next of the 1805 exhibitors worth individual attention, was a theatrical scene-painter. In 1741 there was a Thomas Dixon who worked as a glazier in St Peter Mancroft, and in 1841 a John Dixon worked as a glass-painter in the same church, of which he was churchwarden. Robert was probably of this family. He was born in Norwich in 1780, but by some means trained at the Royal Academy where he exhibited *Design for a Ceiling* in 1798 and was described as an architect. He was in Norwich again in 1801 for he was employed at the Theatre there as a scene-painter. The Theatre had been rearranged and redecorated according to the plans of William Wilkins, and if, as is probable, Dixon did some of the decorating, he was in Norwich by 1800. Dickes says that he was pressed to accept employment in London by William Capon. This is perhaps a clue to Dixon's early training and the means whereby he got to London and the Royal Academy in the first place.

To the Norwich Society Exhibition of 1805 Dixon contributed fifteen pictures, all landscapes or drawings of architectural exteriors, and probably all water-colours. Of these one, *Near Magdalen Gates*, is now in Norwich Castle. Although it is signed it is not dated, but as a larger and more elaborate version also in Norwich Castle, is dated 1809 (Cot. and Haw., page 111, Plate 4) it is reasonable to suppose that the smaller and earlier is the drawing of this title shown in 1805. These two pictures, and others like them, such as that in Mr Geoffrey Allen's collection (Plate 23b), and a very large one in the Whitworth, are broadly conceived, broadly executed water-colours in strong tones and rather rich plum-like colouring. They display all the merits one would expect of a theatrical scene-painter and of a glass-painter whose job it is to be effective at a distant view, but they lack subtlety and tenderness.

Dixon's contribution to the 1806 exhibition contained six landscapes or portraits of buildings and five rather unusual pieces: two *Imitations of Bronze*, two called *Cupid Benighted*, and a *Head of Laocoon*. The first two suggest the theatrical scene-painter working at *trompe l'oeil*.

The last, but probably not the youngest, of these early leaders of the School is Charles Hodgson. His dates are not established, but as his son David Hodgson was born in 1798, and as he last exhibited in 1825, we shall not be far out if we date his birth in the 1770s. There is a splendid landscape in gouache by him in Norwich Castle dated 1797 (Plate 5b) of which Iolo Williams was unreasonably critical. This seems to relate to Robert Ladbrooke's *Norfolk Broad* (Plate 15b); a similarity which may provide a clue to the identification of more of Hodgson's work.

Charles Hodgson exhibited at the Royal Academy four times between 1802 and 1824. In 1802 he kept a boarding-school and later became Mathematical Master at the Norwich Free School. Also, like Crome, Ladbrooke, and Dixon he set up as a drawing-master. The Norwich gouache is rather French in manner, a little like a Moucheron, and has a somewhat sophisticated air in consequence; if his other work is in this vein it would easily escape recognition as a Norwich product.

These five men, Crome, Ladbrooke, Dixon, Thirtle, and Hodgson were the main support of the Society's first two exhibitions, but in 1807 they were joined by one who was not only an immeasurably greater water-colourist than the last four but who was also one of the most original and sensitive artists ever to work in England.

John Sell Cotman (1782–1842) was born in Norwich the son of a barber who later became a draper. In the autumn of 1798 at the age of $16\frac{1}{2}$ he was working at Ackerman's art factory in the Strand. There he probably coloured prints and made himself generally useful, but left before long because he thought Ackerman 'failed to treat him as he ought'. According to the account of his son, Miles Edmund, he was 'taken by the late Dr Monro, with whom he remained some time, studying with Turner and Girtin'. Kitson points out that this must be wrong as Cotman is unlikely to have been at Monro's until 1799 by which time Turner and Girtin had ceased to work there. Probably Cotman began to frequent Monro's house as soon as he arrived in London in the autumn of 1798, and Turner and Girtin, although on a different footing, may have been met with there long after their so-called 'pupillage' ended. In any event living and working under the eye of Monro it was impossible that he should not become acquainted with the only two water-colourists whose names are commonly thought to rank with his.

Cotman alone amongst the leading Norwich men was fully exposed to metropolitan influences on the highest level at the beginning of his career. As a young man he moved amongst the most talented water-colourists of his day. Influences are rarely one way and the web of interacting work and opinion is too complex even for those involved to understand. Cotman had an original, vivid, and fluent personality, and almost certainly influenced some of his seniors quite as much as they did him. The measure of his stature is that the Sketching Club which had gathered around Girtin became known after Girtin's death as Cotman's Drawing Society though he was perhaps the youngest member of it.

The Sketching Club was typical of a time when artists were constantly grouping themselves for the exchange of ideas and the forwarding of their art and may have grown naturally out of the meeting of young artists at Dr Monro's. It was an association of a few water-colourists who met first in May 1799 under the name of The Brothers, and proclaimed as their purpose 'establishing by practice a School of Historic Landscape—the subjects being designs from poetick passages'. These young men assembled regularly in each other's rooms where they sketched for three hours, working on a subject selected by their host and based on a passage from a poem. They then supped modestly and discussed their work over a tankard of ale. Cotman was not an original member of the group but he was certainly a member at the same time as Girtin, probably in 1800.

It is clear that at the outset these, the *avant-garde* of their day, did not consider that landscape painting should limit itself to the recording of fact but rather that things seen should provide the raw material from which great historical landscapes could be constructed. This sort of demand was constantly being made towards the end of the eighteenth and throughout the nineteenth centuries; a demand which assumed the superiority of the subject picture to all other kinds.[1] It was especially the demand of the generation that matured during the romantic attitudinizing of the Napoleonic Wars, who in their architecture and their furniture, in their literature and their music, and sometimes in their lives, cultivated grandeur. In literature its most typical products were the novels of Scott and the poems of Byron; in painting it brought forth numberless *Deaths of Nelson* and *Hannibals crossing the Alps*, a type of picture which has generally filled with dismay the *cognoscenti* of the first half of the twentieth century—a dismay which is unlikely to be echoed so whole-heartedly when another thirty years are past. But Scott and the historical subject picture were only one aspect of Romanticism; another aspect lay in the

---

[1] Sir Thomas Lawrence considered Constable 'peculiarly fortunate in being chosen an Academician at a time when there were historical painters of great merit on the list of candidates'. C. R. Leslie, *Memoirs of the Life of John Constable.*

mystical relationship of man to his natural surroundings, the romanticism of Words-worth's *Ode on the Intimations of Immortality*, of Collins's *Ode to Evening*. Despite the avowed purpose of the Sketch Club to establish a School of Historic Landscape it fortunately did no such thing, but it *did* keep before these young painters of landscape the idea that something more than the record of a thing seen was required, that by the fire of poetic imagination the thing seen could be transferred into a work of art, that landscape by itself although it told no story could move a beholder to sensations equal to those which the literary imagination aroused. The effect of the 'Drawing Society' was undoubtedly to initiate Cotman's art in a direction quite different from that taken by Crome.

In 1800 Cotman exhibited six drawings at the Royal Academy (Plate 28a) and in the same year was awarded 'the Large Silver Palette by the Society for the encouragement of Arts, Manufactures and Commerce' for a drawing of a mill. This is probably the water-colour in the Fitzwilliam Museum (Plate 30a).[1] The colour of both this and the picture at Doncaster Museum is a prevailing reddish brown and their treatment is rather hard. The 'red-brown' period (not, I think, entirely owing to the flight of blue pigment as Oppé supposed) must have been very brief because a drawing of the Cow Tower at Norwich Castle in this distinctive hue also exists in a larger and far finer version in a full 'blue period' manner dated 1801 in the collection of Mr S. Rowland Pierce.

His progress from this point was quick. If the *Water-Mill* contains little of the essential Cotman the work done on his journeys to Wales in 1800 and 1802 contains much. Like most young water-colourists of his day he came under the influence of Girtin and began to see his own work as an extension of the qualities peculiar to his medium in a way Crome would never have done. As Oppé wrote of him—'Conspicuously on his side, in our eyes, is his sense of the actual drawing or painting as a thing of artistic and emo-tional value in its colour, line and massing over and above, or at best, through and through, the significance of the objects represented'.[2]

Cotman's awareness of the picture as an object with its own independent life became apparent on his first Welsh trip, although the manner of creation was still not purely his own but Girtin's. It is from this tour and the drawings which immediately relate to it that we must date the beginning of Cotman's incomparable 'blue period' water-colours (Plates 28b, 29a, 29b). At the same time running through the more obviously derivative work of these early years can be discerned the beginnings of his own highly personal style. There is often a sort of Chinese delicacy in his washes which it may not be altogether

---

[1] Kitson suggests that the 'palette' picture may be the *Mill* now in Norwich Castle but this hardly seems of prize-winning quality.
[2] *The Water-Colour Drawings of John Sell Cotman:* The Studio, 1923.

fanciful to see as reminiscent of Crome's grey-wash drawings. From these he progressively developed a curious formalism, a sort of schematic rendering of shapes which developed eventually into almost pure pattern-making.

The distinguishing characteristic of Cotman's first fully individual manner was his use of washes to build up a picture in broad tonal planes rather as a stage set is built, flat behind flat. Light and shadow are not used in the normal way to give solidity to objects or recession to the landscape, but rather in order to create a satisfying pattern upon the surface of the paper. The effect, as has been often remarked, is oddly like that of the great Japanese woodcuts which became familiar in Europe at the end of the nineteenth century but could hardly have been known to Cotman.

There are several possible sources of this manner. The first is intellectual, and as Cotman was fundamentally an intellectual aesthete, this must be important. All art involves the elimination of inessentials—it remains only to determine which are essentials. No one, for example, can paint every leaf in a tree. They can, like Glover, seek to give the impression that they are doing so, or like most artists adopt a formula which will enable people to accept that the tree is in fact largely compounded of leaves. Cotman frankly resolves the tree into its main masses and delineates them as shapes only, making usually little and often no attempt to persuade the viewer that they are masses of leaves. The essential aesthetic effect is obtained, according to this way of thinking, by the shape and disposition of the masses. They are not trees, they are 'enchanted bath-sponges'—but they have a value in the picture parallel to that which trees have in the landscape.

Cotman's months spent at Ackerman's colouring prints may have helped to suggest to him this simplification of vision. Probably his work there was to wash in areas with colour in the way which would most quickly give an effect. The consequence to young artists of learning their trade from prints and working on them has been too little considered, although anyone who looks at, for example, the engraving of the Waldegrave Poussin by Mason must see how much it has lent to Cotman's *The Devil's Elbow* (Plate 51a).

Mr Graham Reynolds has suggested that Cotman was influenced by Joshua Cristall.[1] Although Cristall was fifteen years older than Cotman he also had been befriended by Dr Monro, and Cotman will have known both the man and his work because of this common contact. There is certainly something in Cristall's bold simplification of forms and the way in which he organized those forms into patterns which is reminiscent of Cotman, but Cristall's work which can be dated before 1805 does not have this characteristic and he almost certainly acquired it from the younger man. More obvious and no less probable

[1] *An Introduction to English Water-Colour Painting* by Graham Reynolds, 1950.

is a debt to Francis Towne. Towne's drawings were not widely known in their day but an exhibition of nearly two hundred of them was held in London in Lower Brook Street in 1805. We should perhaps in both these cases look less to direct influence than to a similar response to common stimuli.

At another level there was considerable give and take between Cotman and John Varley. Varley was a man of inquiring mind, of alarming activity, and of a fluent expansive nature, the very type of man most likely to influence Cotman and the type most likely to be influenced by him. From their common base in Girtin their paths are close between 1803 and 1808; at about that date, though both deepened their palettes, they diverge until 1822 when Varley stayed at Yarmouth with the Dawson Turners (Plate 27b). Throughout his life Varley was liable to be less scrupulous a draughtsman than Cotman and better able to appeal to contemporary tastes, but they have more in common with each other than either has with his fellows of comparable achievement.[1]

Superficially closer to Cotman's work than those we have mentioned was for a short time Paul Sandby Munn. Munn is misjudged by many people because of some tight, finely executed pencil drawings made in the '20s and '30s which are rather dull. But the earlier Munn, though he may have lacked an artistic personality strong enough to create a form of expression peculiar to himself, always added to the current manner that touch of feminine delicacy which stamps his work. He and Cotman travelled together in Wales and in Yorkshire, and for some time Cotman lodged in his house. Munn's less well-known early work often shows a likeness to Cotman's and it is reasonable to suppose that something at least of the common factor was Munn's contribution (Plate 26a).

Nevertheless, although these men and perhaps many others contributed to Cotman's development they retained no dominion over him; the artist who swiftly emerged from their company was one of the most original and individual ever to appear in Western art.

In 1803 Cotman, travelling in Yorkshire with Munn, was taken up by Mr and Mrs Cholmeley of Brandsby Hall. With them he spent that summer and to Brandsby he returned in the two succeeding years. It is not difficult to believe that these summers were the happiest of Cotman's life. The Cholmeleys, great landowners, moved in a circle of culture and wealth, and took the young artist with them not as a humble drawing-master of semi-menial status but as a friend. He was young and he was admired and liked by a family which had unaffectedly introduced him to a milieu where he felt himself expand, a milieu which his appearance, his talents, and his own notion of his ancestry, made him feel was naturally his. The result of this happy period was a number of great

[1] *See* Appendix 'C'.

drawings of which the cream were those produced in the vicinity of Rokeby Park and the River Greta.

The style of every artist is *au fond* the result of his inability to record accurately his vision; the compromise, conscious or unconscious, involves the development of a species of shorthand, which may derive entirely from the practice of other artists or may be to a considerable degree a personal solution. The personal solution reflects the essential artist and is his 'style'. If the solution appeals to his contemporaries (because his requirements basically answer theirs) he is a popular artist; if his character is not the character of the age he will fail.

The personal style that Cotman evolved during the years between 1800 and 1805 was in a real sense severely classical. His draughtsmanship was firm and assured, his colour-sense was restrained and sensitive, his handling of washes was miraculously controlled, and his composition was deliberate and inevitable. The best drawings of this period are of the order of a Sung bowl, a Minoan seal, an Attic vase, a marble of the fifth century B.C. (Plate 31a). These are not arts of the market-place and nor was his. Despite the fact that he was quickly known to most of the leading patrons and connoisseurs of his day they seem not to have cultivated him. Sir George Beaumont gave him no encouragement; Sir Henry Englefield, to whom he hopefully dedicated a book of engravings, seems to have bought little of his work;[1] the Marquess of Stafford to whose home he went as drawing-master replaced him by Peter de Wint within a month. He showed at the Royal Academy and found no purchasers. In 1804 the Water-Colour Society was founded but he was not among the members.

In July 1806 Mr Cholmeley wrote to him: 'I am grieved and surprised at your want of success far more than I can express, and can only anxiously hope that if any defects in your Stile of Drawing have a share in causing it, you will have Will and Perseverance, as you certainly have Power to correct these faults . . . you ought to know by my example that yr. *best friends* criticise you the most *severely*. 'Tis your good only I have uniformly sought in saying things to you I knew would give you offence, but you have too often found I was right in my advice when, believe me, I had far rather have been wrong than you should! . . . You will now perhaps, dear Cotty, be angry when I tell you that I wish your last letter had been a little more quiet and sober. Your joy seems to me foolishly extravagant for a very precarious advantage. It will give me *real Joy indeed* to find everything answers your Expectations there, but Alas! how few events in Life ever do this, and therefore we should always be armed against disappointment which your

---

[1] There are, however, distinct signs of Cotman's influence in one of Englefield's drawings in the possession of Mr and Mrs Cyril Fry; and he certainly subscribed for Cotman's publications.

ardent sanguine Spirit I fear rarely is. . . . Farewell, and Heaven bless and direct you, my dear Cotty. Whether prosperous or unlucky signifies nothing in my regard for you. Be virtuous, be steady, and nothing can influence the friendship and affection of yr. friends here towards you. God bless you, dear Cotty, and "forget me not".'

Cotman, despite the brilliant promise of his early career, failed to achieve the sort of success his nature required. The same was true of many of his contemporaries, but their need for success—their material, spiritual, and social requirements—was very often less than his. The greater tragedy of Cotman was that he was unable to work as so many others did for subsistence only. He was a manic-depressive and alternated between moods of extravagant hope which went with vivid activity, and periods of utter gloom and despair during which work was impossible to him. Faced with this fearful mental imbalance he went through his life with extraordinary courage and persistence and wrung from it, if not the applause of his contemporaries, certainly the admiration of posterity.

The warmth of love and admiration which the Cholmeley family clearly felt for him he never found again. His last visit to Brandsby was in 1805. Mr Cholmeley died in 1808, and his wife in 1810, leaving Cotman a small legacy. There is some advice that cannot be taken and Cotman's 'ardent, sanguine Spirit' was never, in fact, able to arm itself against disappointment.

During these years, of which the highlights were his summer excursions to Wales and Yorkshire, he did not lose touch with Norwich but visited his father there, made the acquaintance of Dawson Turner, and sketched amongst the ruins of East Anglia. Then, in 1807, against all probability, he made a remarkable decision: he left London and settled in Norwich to establish a School of Drawing and Design.

Cotman's style had so far shown consistent development from the academic *An Overshot Mill* (Plate 30a), through the dramatic blue period of *Brecknock* (Plate 28b), to the increased formalizing of his material in the 'Greta' drawings (Plate 31a). In Yorkshire he had consciously set himself to do colour studies from nature, and though we may feel that these exquisite harmonies are rarely what we now understand as natural colouring, they are, in fact, observed colour relationships—they are the *sort* of colours Cotman found in nature though disciplined and related in his own way. By comparison with what had gone before these are Cotman's colours and not the colours of studio convention, nor had they yet been reduced to a convention of his own. From the date of his settling in Norwich until 1812 we can see that steady increase in formalization both of pattern and colour which inevitably follows over-production of studio work. For the first year or two the colours he discovered in Yorkshire remained with him, but he used them now increasingly

Plate III *The Mill, Eye, Suffolk* John Sell Cotman (1782–1842)

and most successfully for drawings of church interiors. Many of the water-colours of the period reflect that interest in decayed gothic architecture which was shortly to topple him over into antiquarianism, but they remain amongst his greatest achievements. In this direction he could go no farther. Gradually the 'Greta' delicacies were replaced by strongly contrasted tones and rich pulsating colours that became an eye-catching formula, which though superb in such drawings as *The Marl Pit* (Plate 32b) can sometimes be a little tiresome.

Cotman first appeared at the Exhibition of the Norwich Society in 1807 with twenty exhibits, of which six were portraits, and he now described himself as 'Portrait Painter'. In 1809 he is still so described but after that year he showed no more portraits and presumably accepted the fact that portraiture, save at Court level, was uneconomic.

During this first Norwich period 1807–12 Cotman was much occupied with painting in oils, and if his oils sometimes show signs of being the conception of a water-colourist his water-colours begin to take on some of the qualities of oils. This was characteristic of the time and not at all peculiar to Cotman. The antagonism between painters in the two mediums which had contributed to the formation of the Water Colour Society arose partly from the fact that water-colours did not show well when hung in the company of oils. This the water-colourists set about correcting and it became common practice to deepen tonality and thicken the quality of the paint so that water-colours like oils could take the heavy gold frames which the rules of the Old Water Colour Society demanded.[1] In Cotman's work of this period the broad flat washes remain, the construction is increasingly strong, the colour becomes rich and plummy. Splendidly effective though it usually is, we are now conscious of being in the presence of something slightly less than genius, of drawings which strike at first sight but wear a little less well. Cotman had in fact found a formula just as Varley at the same time had done and, though the drawings he produced with it were usually superior to Varley's, similar signs of over-production are there; taste and talent remain, but the passionate involvement that made so many of the Yorkshire drawings unequalled works of art rarely appears. It had not, however, gone for ever and in the meantime these run-of-the-mill Cotmans are splendid by any standards but his own.

As his marriage in 1809 made it necessary to earn more money than he was able to do from the sale of pictures he intensified his efforts to find pupils. Crome, Ladbrooke, Hodgson, and Thirtle were already in the field but Cotman sought to attract clients by the novelty of his approach. He established a circulating library of drawings which subscribers

[1] John Varley was an outstanding example of this tendency, which probably contributed to his popularity.

of one guinea a quarter could borrow and copy. This is the explanation of the numbers which so often appear on the front of Cotman drawings.[1]

In 1810 he sent four oils to London to the British Institution and ten water-colours to the Associated Painters in Water-colours—a rival to the society that he had strangely not joined in 1804. Neither exhibition did him any good and their immediate result was that he dropped oil-painting for the time being, confined his water-colouring to little else than necessary drawing copies, and devoted himself with typical whole-heartedness to etching architectural antiquities. In 1812, under pressure from Dawson Turner, banker-antiquarian, he moved to Yarmouth to become drawing-master to Mrs Turner and her daughters, and for the next twelve years to produce for his patron great numbers of detailed architectural drawings.[2]

[1] Low numbers generally indicate a date about 1809 and 1810 but sometimes a lost or worn-out drawing was replaced much later and bears a misleadingly early number. The first 600 were available in 1809. Many of the later numbers—those above 2,000—were done by other members of his family and signed by him; numbers below 2,000 are nearly always by Cotman himself. This is not the explanation, however, of certain numbers which are occasionally to be found on the back of highly-finished water-colours which could not conceivably have been used as drawing copies. These are low numbers and probably relate to some exhibition or private catalogue which Cotman planned.

[2] There is some evidence that he met Dawson Turner through first having taught Mrs Turner before her marriage.

3

The Middle Period (a) 1812-24

URING COTMAN'S first Norwich period several young men who were later to become leading Norwich artists made their début at the Society's exhibitions. They were the harbingers of the second generation of the Norwich School and, though their earliest works were sometimes juvenilia of little importance, they became during the years of Cotman's absence in Yarmouth the hard core of the School.

The senior was Henry Ninham (1793–1874), son of that minor precursor of the movement, John Ninham, who drew the series of City Gates. The father was an engraver and heraldic-painter and the son was trained to the same trade. Unlike so many of his fellows who were experienced exhibitors in their 'teens Ninham did not begin to show until 1816 and then very little; during fifteen years there were only sixteen exhibits in his name. Nevertheless Ninham's work is fairly common in and around Norwich for he was a new type of topographer—the portraitist of cottage, shop, and inn rather than of church and mansion—and there must have been a ready market for such things (Plate 42a). Most of his pictures are in oil and his water-colours are no more than versions of the oils, although a few exist with a more genuine landscape character which show greater talent than he deployed later (Plate 42b). As a draughtsman his most notable achievement is said to have been a full-face peacock the size of a shilling. His topographical work is not as meticulous as this triumph suggests, but to me at least these drawings are lacking in ease and breadth. His colour is quietly distinctive though not distinguished, its usual range based upon a pearly grey and a soft grey-green. Certainly not a major artist, Ninham has the virtue which few Norwich artists lack, personal modesty in front of his subject.

The next to appear was John Berney Crome (1794–1842), the eldest son of John Crome, and the reason why his father is known to posterity as 'Old' Crome. His first contribution to the Society's Exhibition in 1806 actually preceded Cotman's by a year; he was then a boy of 12. He exhibited again in 1808 and at the Royal Academy in 1811 at the age of 17. He appears to have been a sociable, flamboyant man, fond of drink and company. As an oil painter he followed his father—at a considerable distance—but specialized in those moonlight scenes in the manner of Van der Neer which ultimately became his standard 'best selling line'. As a water-colourist he is difficult to identify. Our usually firm foundation, the Reeve Collection in the British Museum, contains one only, a bold, un-subtle view of a tower against a late evening sky. One of the remaining three is signed and, were it not, it would be given to Sillett or any other careful fruit and flower painter. The others are over-elaborate drawing-master's pencil work of the worst sort. At Norwich Castle there is a small water-colour given to him which, in the absence of contrary indica-tions, we should accept. It is a distant view of Yarmouth beach with shipping faintly visible on the horizon and a serried line of windmills stretching into the distance. Its delicate colouring gives it a jewel-like quality (Plate 43a). But where are others like it? In Yarmouth Library there is another small water-colour well-authenticated as done in 1840, which is less good (Plate 43b). There is also a copy of it by Miss Brightwell made in 1862[1] which is much superior to the original. Two monochromes in Mr L. G. Duke's collection—one of them signed—are not without merit although in comparison with his father's work they are rather hard. Two water-colours called *Views of Norwich* were in Sir Henry Holmes collection in 1932.[2] There are also a fair number of pencil drawings about, almost uniformly bad, either dry and scratchy or painfully laboured. It is difficult to believe that the creator of these drawings produced much worth attention.

A third newcomer of very different calibre was James Stark (1794–1859), who ex-hibited two *Pencil Studies after Crome* in 1809. In 1811 he was apprenticed to Crome and became, professionally, the most successful of his followers. He was a member of the Society in 1812, and though in 1814 he moved his headquarters for some years to London he often returned to his home town and exhibited there. Stark, like his friend J. B. Crome, was chiefly a painter in oils but he seems to have sketched a good deal and produced a number of finished pictures in water-colour. There are nineteen examples in the British Museum and he is represented in several public and private collections.

Stark's water-colour work is in general free, incisive, and unfinished. It suggests speed rather than care and has a sharply defined linear character, rarely to be found at an early date. He was particularly fond of drawing young oaks which are at times a shade too elegant in form. He is not a Water-Colour Society type of water-colourist nor is he a particularly fluent sketcher, but it may be by way of him that a new 'break' in water-colour developed. If so he was the principal link between the founder-members of the

[1] Miss Lucy Brightwell (1811–25), a skilled copyist of whom Cotman wrote that her 'copy of Rembrandt's *Mill* is most astonishingly etched and more like Rembrandt than anything I have ever seen'.
[2] Catalogue of the Holmes Collection, privately printed 1932.

Norwich School and its autumnal flowering in Bright and Middleton. Again we are handi-capped by lack of dated material and it may be that if the majority of Starks are from his later years he learned from Bright and Middleton rather than they from him. However, I believe this is unlikely; there are several reasons for thinking them relatively early, and if so we must regard Stark as the first step in the fusion of the tradition of Crome with the tradition of Cotman. His vision is that of his master Crome but the clear colours, the broad and simple washes, are the appropriate virtues of the medium, and this is a Cotman not a Crome characteristic. Direct Cotman influence we do not find; nor should we expect it, for Stark's formative years at Norwich coincided with Cotman's Yarmouth period. Later indeed they must have been associated for Stark constantly visited Norwich and was President of the Norwich Society in 1830.

Stark's water-colours are not commonly of the sort much framed and hung, so that they have existed in portfolios and have the advantage of unfaded freshness. Unfor-tunately he was addicted to the use of coloured papers (a characteristic of the 1820s—though not confined to them) and his colour often fails of that brilliance which white paper would have given (Plates 44a–46b).

Yet another newcomer was George Vincent (1796–1831) who was also a pupil of Crome and a friend of his son. He and John Berney Crome visited France together in 1816. His life was not successful, debt and an unfortunate marriage may have caused him to put an end to it, but he is sometimes said to have had a greater and more original talent than Stark. There are eight drawings by him in the British Museum, three of them from the Reeve Collection, and Mr Harold Day has a considerable run of them, all of Scottish subjects and dated 1831. As drawings they seem at first glance undistinguished; they are jumpy and unco-ordinated in line and their chief virtue is in their lack of sophistication. Vincent seems always to be reaching out after a delicacy of conception which his execution could not support. His pencil drawings, I believe, are sometimes mistaken for Cromes. I have seen few of his water-colours. In the Loan Exhibition organized by the Society of British Artists in 1832 there was only one picture listed as a water-colour, *The Needles from Christchurch*. This is the picture in Norwich Castle signed GV 1830 (Plate 48a). It is a pleasant piece of work to which the underlying jumpiness of the drawing gives vitality. In the 1927 Exhibition at Norwich Castle there was a signed and dated water-colour of *Sandling Ferry* of which the present whereabouts are unknown. Norwich Castle also con-tains a picture hitherto attributed to Joseph Stannard but which is similar to *The Needles* picture and is certainly by Vincent (Plate 48b). In the National Gallery, Washington, there is a water-colour seascape rather more free than either of those at Norwich, and two line and wash drawings, of which one is certainly by Vincent and the other, rather more coarse and bold in treatment, a possible early work. Two other Vincents I have seen are Scottish mountain landscapes. One was shown by Appleby Brothers in 1963 and is now in the possession of Mr Harold Day (Plate 49a); the other is in my own collection (Plate 49b). These are quite unlike *The Needles* picture in subject and colour but again one can detect the accented drawing behind them. Vincents' death in 1831 has long been suspect, though why it should have become traditional to doubt it is not clear; in the absence of positive evidence we should accept the ostensible date as correct. Unlike most of the Norwich men Vincent took regular sketching tours outside East Anglia, many of them in Scotland, which may account for the apparent shortage of water-colours attributed to him, for unless signed they would not immediately suggest a Norwich source.

It would be natural to expect that the appearance in the youthful Norwich Society of so dynamic and personal an artist as Cotman would make itself apparent in the work of others. Some writers assume that this is so. Crome and Thirtle in particular are quoted as having changed their styles under the impact of this Norwich man fresh from London. But the evidence is slight. If we group all Cromes together we easily see a variation in the degree of 'finish' employed. A good example is in the version of *Wood Scene* at Norwich Castle which is more broadly handled than the slightly larger but identical one at the Victoria and Albert. That in London is the earlier. Are we to see Cotman's influence in either? The London picture is a technical advance on two of the *Tinterns* of 1805 but is this anything to do with Cotman? One of the finest of Crome's water-colours, *Houses and Wherries on the Wensum* in the Whitworth Art Gallery (Plate 13), may perhaps be thought to show something of Cotman; but even here, if one is to search for influences, there seems to be rather more of Girtin in it, as there undoubtedly is in another drawing of the same period, the *Near Lakenham* at Norwich Castle (Plate 6a).

Nor is the influence of Cotman on Thirtle often readily recognizable. Thirtle, although the older man, had admired Cotman's work when he was still a boy in London and in 1812 he married Cotman's wife's sister; but I doubt if anyone has ever been in danger of mistaking a Thirtle for a Cotman although, as in the Whitworth's *Old Waterside Cottage, Norwich*, the influence is occasionally very clear. What Thirtle learned from the greater man appears in a touch of drama in his construction, a hint of the Cotman pattern-making; but we rarely see any attempt at reproducing those astonishingly assured and accurate flat washes which were Cotman's peculiar gift.

The truth is that there was really very little common ground between Crome and his followers and Cotman and his. Crome was an objective painter and cultivated the appearance of being more objective than he was. Cotman was subjective, as personal in his calm way as Blake or Samuel Palmer. In its early, undiluted, austere form Cotman's style could only be copied; few could digest it for few shared his purpose.

Where Cotman's influence may have been great was in setting a higher standard of technical accomplishment in the Norwich Exhibition than it had previously known, and in demonstrating that water-colour need not be unequal in strength to oil.

And here we find ourselves close again to the work of Robert Dixon which, from the different starting-point of scene-painting, arrived at similarly bold effects. But there seems no reason to see Cotman's influence in these 'back-cloth' pictures by Dixon, and in the few later Dixons which can be identified this element instead of increasing has lessened. Dixon is said to have died on 1 October 1815, at the age of 35, and to have exhibited nowhere but with the Norwich Society, and there only during its first six years. This, however, is contradicted by a notice in the *Norwich Chronicle* which in 1830 speaks of his reappearance, calls him 'of London', and refers to his variety in subject: compositions, figures, and architecture; and to his affinity to Westall. Some biographical research is required, for this is presumably another Dixon, perhaps his son. In the meantime it is better to assume that the date of his obituary is correct.[1] Among his exhibited work there were latterly several titles which suggest that he was engaged on book illustrations, which may have absorbed his time and prevented his exhibiting after 1810. Later he showed signs of freeing himself from the fetters of his stage-painting past and developing a more free and expressive manner. Had he continued in the way of his *Fisherman's Cottages* (Plate 25a), his name would now stand higher than it does. Iolo Williams was so impressed with the quality of this drawing that he found it difficult to believe that it was by Dixon, despite a Reeve attribution and a provenance from Dixon's son. Yet other sketches by him, although they lack the gentleness and atmosphere of this, show him capable of sensitivity. But these late sketches suggest that he was beginning to relax his manner not under the influence of Cotman but of Crome. Robert Ladbrooke alone of the older members of the Society may have attempted to emulate in part Cotman's simplification of form, but he never achieved washes as consummate as the younger master's and his sense of colour was far behind; as whose was not?

While these men were establishing themselves at Norwich, Cotman from 1812 until 1823 was working with his usual hectic intensity on a series of architectural drawings and etchings at Yarmouth. These twelve years were sadly unfruitful of great water-colours. We are probably right to date the last of the dark 'plummy' toned pictures to the year of the removal to Yarmouth and to date the beginning of the sepias to 1817, when he made his first trip to Normandy, but the years between held nothing but the production of

[1] *Norfolk Chronicle*—October, 1815.

architectural plates which poured from him at the rate of one a fortnight, whilst at the same time he gave interminable drawing lessons to the women of the Turner family.

The pursuit of architectural material to feed to Dawson Turner for use in his researches led him to Normandy in 1817, in 1818, and again in 1820. These resulted in the publication (1820–23) of *Architectural Antiquities of Normandy*, in which Cotman's plates illustrated his patron's text. At first Cotman's natural leanings towards antiquarianism threw him whole-heartedly into the work, but as eventually Dawson Turner's hobby changed from discovering the origins of Gothic architecture to collecting autograph letters, Cotman rebelled against the need to make factual drawings only and began to allow himself to see again as an artist and not as a *camera lucida*. Though artistic merit was not required of these drawings they never fell below a high level of competence and often have a more positive quality, although in many of them the mechanical means leaves a certain unsympathetic starkness. Now and again throughout his Normandy tours, and particularly during the last, the artistic vision swamps the antiquarian and some superlative drawings result. Some of the best of these were designed for a book on *Picturesque Normandy* which, like so many of Cotman's projects, died for want of encouragement.

It was Cotman's practice to do pencil drawings in the field but to work these up with washes later in the studio. Few of the Normandy drawings reached the stage of full watercolour but many of them exist in sepia (Plate 35b), and it is remarkable to see how the bare linear records of his drawings were given solidity, depth, lighting, and mood, with a few simple washes, for the placing of which no hint appears upon the original drawings at all. Nothing contributes so much to the strongly marked individuality of Cotman's picture-making as his arbitrary disposal of shadow. The laws of light he largely disregards and though he generally disposes his shadows so that they all fall away from the source of light, he varies their tonal depth entirely in accordance with the demands of his pattern. This is particularly apparent in the sepia drawings which resulted from the later Normandy journeys.

From 1812 until about 1818 Cotman did virtually no coloured drawings and when he resumed colour practice it was in a manner peculiar to himself. This was the beginning of his much-debated Gold-and-Blue Period. It has been suggested that his adoption of so striking a palette was in emulation of Turner's success in a similar direction. But in fact there is little similarity in the approach of the two men to the problem, and Cotman's new colour scheme is far more likely to have been based upon a little book published by Ackerman, his old employer, in 1817 and dedicated to the Governor and Directors of the British Institution. This was *Daylight: a recent Discovery in the Art of Painting with Hints on the Philosophy of the Fine Arts and on that of the Human Mind as first dissected by*

Plate IV *Snowdon from Capel Curig* Robert Leman (1799–1863)

Emanuel Kant, by Henry Richter. In it the author imagines himself to be looking at the collection of Old Master paintings shown at the British Institution and to be surrounded by the shades of the Masters themselves. In a colloquy with Teniers he ways 'Was there no clear sky in your day, and did not the broad blue light of the atmosphere shine then, as it does now. . . .? And this light from the sky should fall perpendicularly upon the tops of all objects, whether the sun shines upon them or not. I find, in nature, it is *this* which gives the chief splendour of sunshine, by contrasting the *golden* with the *azure* light.' From about 1818 until nearly the end of his life the idea of the 'splendour of sunshine' represented by the contrast of 'golden and azure light' is rarely absent from Cotman's water-colours.

John Crome, who seems to have been instrumental in Cotman's removal to Yarmouth by his unwillingness to continue teaching the Turner girls and his refusal to enter into that domineering man's antiquarian schemes, had in the meanwhile pursued his way with quiet success in Norwich, popular as a teacher, as an artist, and as a man. In 1814 the end of the war with France gave him and many other British artists an opportunity to see the looted pictures in the Louvre. This trip, which was so much in character as to resemble a schoolboy's jaunt rather than a sketching tour, resulted in some oil-paintings remarkably different in content from any he had done before.

It is possible, partly by means of this journey, to distinguish a later style in a few of Crome's water-colours. In Norwich Castle there is a small picture, *Silver Birches* (Plate 14a), copied from the corner of an oil-painting by Adam Pynacker which is in Dulwich College Gallery. Dulwich Gallery was opened in 1814 and Crome almost certainly copied the picture on his journey to Paris.[1] It is an attractive drawing but naturally has little of Crome's breadth; it is also more highly coloured than usual. *Trees by Water* (Plate 14b), a copy of the centre of Cuyp's *Evening Ride Near a River* in the same Gallery, connects with this because, although the colour has entirely changed to russet, a similar technique of wiping-out has been employed on the foliage. Probably the last of all Crome's water-colours, related to an oil on which he was working when he died, is *Wroxham Regatta* in Norwich Castle (Kaines Smith, page 60: *Burlington Magazine*, July-August 1959, fig. 49). This drawing has been much admired but I do not find in it the qualities which make so many of Crome's pictures a moving experience.

The only other event to disturb the routine of his life was a disagreement on policy

[1] This seems to be a reasonable guess. Mr Francis Hawcroft, however, in *The Connoiseur*, December 1959, p. 236, prefers an earlier date and implies that Crome may have seen the Pynacker in the Harvey Collection at Catton. The identification of *Trees by Water* supports my view, but both pictures *may* have been at Catton.

which resulted in a schism of The Norwich Society. In 1816 Robert Ladbrooke led away a secessionist body which called itself The Norfolk and Norwich Society of Artists and included, among the older members of the Society, Sillett and Thirtle. This group exhibited for only three years and then collapsed, but the division lessened for a time the Norwich artists' collective strength.

Then in 1821 at the age of 53 Crome died, leaving behind him an image and a myth larger than the man himself. Whatever sincerity and a determined avoidance of the posturings of art could achieve he had achieved. As a painter in oils he has been written of as greater than Hobbema, Claude, Ruysdael, and Constable.[1] He has been likened to Velasquez. Today, though his work is greatly admired, these estimates would not all be endorsed, but familiarity with his rare water-colours makes it clear that in that medium in which he is so little known he is one of the four or five artists who have achieved greatness. The romanticizing journalists of the nineteenth century over-praised the artist but over-simplified the man. We are shown a stolid, honest type of convivial peasant and asked to believe that this figure was Crome. Such men do not paint such pictures. Crome was cheerful and unassuming, qualities that make for popularity. His funeral was attended by an 'immense concourse of people' who 'bore grateful testimony to the estimation in which his character was generally held'. His old pupils came from London to do him honour. All this points to a lovable character, but it does not necessarily point to a simple one.

In fact a close study of Crome's work taken as a whole leaves a certain uneasiness in the mind. Even when one has eliminated all the undoubted forgeries and misattributed works there is left an accumulation of material so at variance with itself that the impression is not of a developing art which one could understand—but of a fluctuating personality that only rarely achieved its moments of synthesis. With this impression it comes as no surprise, although perhaps as a shock, to find that one of Crome's sons was insane.[2]

The estimation in which his pictures were held in his own city may at first seem astonishing. To us, familiar with the work of Constable and the whole development of landscape art in England in the nineteenth century, Crome may not seem an easily distinguishable phenomenon and we may wonder how the 'immense concourse' came to know of him. If, however, we turn to the landscape art which the citizens of Norwich

---

[1] Those who saw his *Cottages on the Wensum* and *Woodland Landscape* hanging in the Mellon Collection at Burlington House in the company of many distinguished Constables will have little difficulty in agreeing with this view.

[2] Crome was twice admitted to hospital in 1793 with hydrocele, one cause of which is tertiary syphilis.

knew before him, to Catton (Plate 1b), to Capon (Plate 2b), to Hodgson (Plate 5b), to John Ninham (Plate 1a) and then turn to Crome's *Wood Scene* (Plate 12c) we shall more easily understand their enthusiasm. Here, in their eyes, was something fresh, an art entirely without 'artiness', an art with no bookish overtones. He was the Chardin of their Norfolk landscape.

Yet it is difficult to escape the impression that Crome was really at the end of a tradition, the last flower of a century which had made Flemish landscape English in the person of Gainsborough, had made Italian landscape English in Wilson, and now completed its achievement by making Dutch landscape English in Crome. As a water-colourist he ranks near Cozens as one of the greatest masters of the eighteenth century; one whose work can more naturally be thought of as growing out of the past than reaching towards the future. Girtin, Turner, and Cotman were of the new age, but Crome was the fruit of the old.

4

The Middle Period (b) 1824-33

WITH THE death of Crome Cotman's prospects of building up a lucrative teaching practice in Norwich in competition with John Berney Crome were much improved. He shook himself free of Dawson Turner with great determination and to Norwich he returned. The Norwich Society to which Cotman came back in 1824 was in several respects not the Society over which he had presided in 1811. Apart from Crome's death and the secession of Ladbrooke there were the new men we have already mentioned growing to maturity and others of the younger generation waiting to be acknowledged.

Of Robert Ladbrooke's three sons who were artists only one has so far appeared as a water-colourist, the youngest, John Berney Ladbrooke (1803–79). His master was said to be Crome, not his father, but this seems unlikely as the quarrel which separated the families occurred when he was 13. This is unfortunately another case where we must construct an image from very flimsy materials. There is a landscape *Below Beddgelert* signed and dated 1852 in Mr Geoffrey Allen's collection (Plate 62b); in the same collection is a *View in Snowdonia* signed but not dated (Plate 63a). There is no difficulty in accepting these as by the same hand, although the second is certainly the earlier and could, had it not been signed, conceivably have been attributed to Robert Ladbrooke. A third alleged J. B. Ladbrooke is in Norwich Castle, *The Team at the Bridge* (Plate 63b). This is neither signed nor dated and reached the Castle under the will of S. R. Kitson. There is no evidence that this is by J. B. Ladbrooke and although the attribution may be correct this picture has greater stylistic congruence with G. Vincent's *The Needles*; there is a similar use of widely scattered dark accents, both dots and lines, in the manner of Vincent's pencil work. This, though perhaps widening our view of Vincent, narrows the foundations on which we can reconstruct J. B. Ladbrooke. Only one water-colour was shown under his name in 1927, *Tintern Abbey*, but this has not reappeared. I have seen several tight pencil drawings by him in emulation of steel engraving, and Mr A. Fellows has a signed monochrome wash drawing; but even allowing for the fact that J. B. Ladbrooke's 76 years were largely spent in oil-painting there should be more than this attributable to him.

If George Vincent and J. B. Ladbrooke are somewhat shadowy figures Joseph Stannard (1797–1830) is one of the best-known members of the School; yet he too has a rather uncertain personality as a water-colourist. He was apprenticed to Robert Ladbrooke so that his early life ran parallel to that of James Stark, the apprentice of Crome. When Ladbrooke seceded Stannard went with him, but when the secessionist group failed he returned at once to the original Society. In 1821 he went to Holland and in 1822 married Emily Coppin (1800–85), the daughter of a member of the Norwich Society who had been with John Crome on his trip to Paris in 1814. Like Stark he was a popular artist but unlike Stark found no need to leave Norwich, where he remained until his early death in 1830.

Stannard is usually considered a painter of seascapes but there are a number of pure landscapes in the list of his exhibits. He was an excellent draughtsman, and his pencil or chalk drawings heightened with a little wash (which are not uncommon) are clear and confident. He was a shining exception to the Norwich landscapists' recognized inability to draw the human figure. There are, however, few pure water-colours that can be attributed convincingly to him. The sensitive *Schooners in a Calm Sea* in Mr S. Rowland Pierce's collection (Plate 51a), is probably by Stannard but has been suggested as the work of William Joy, whom we shall touch on later. The suggestion that Stannard's early work was careful, highly finished, and rather feminine in touch, seems to me inadequately supported and I should prefer to withhold such drawings from him, until convincing evidence appears. Of three water-colours under his name at Norwich Castle one, which is rather jumpy in underlying manner and lacks the suavity of his known wash sketches of figures has now been given to Vincent (Plate 48b) while another (Plate 51b), broader in treatment, despite a faulty horizon level and a general coarseness of handling, is probably by him. *Lugger in a Squall* in my own collection (Plate 50), a brightly-coloured drawing with much body-colour, has the familiar strength and freedom of Stannard's chalk drawings, and the additional advantage of bearing his monogram in the bottom left corner. In 1962 there was a group of Stannard's water-colours and chalk drawings with Mr Frank Sabin. The secret of his sympathies is shown by the fact that whereas Vincent and J. B. Chrome went to France, Stannard journeyed to Holland. As a painter in oils he is more directly related to the Dutch masters than to Crome or Cotman.

Stannard's wife, who survived him by fifty years, was a regular exhibitor of fruit and flower studies in the Van Huysum manner and I have also seen a row of studies of heads after Watteau which are not too far removed from the indescribable elegance of the original. She does not appear to have been an inventive artist but deserves fame if only because of what the *Norwich Mercury* of 1823 said of her: 'she is an honour to art, an honour to the city, and an honour to her sex, by the taste, industry, and knowledge, her beautifully disposed and elaborately finished pictures display. Can we say more? Ought we to have said less?' At this distance of time we can at least agree that her performances are generally above the average of such things.

J. Stannard had a younger brother, Alfred Stannard (1806–89), who in oils worked much in the same manner but finished more laboriously. Though he lived to a considerable age his work is said not to be common. I have seen water-colour sketches which may be by him but nothing that would enable one to assess him as a water-colourist.

Also of the second generation was David Hodgson (1798–1864), son of Charles Hodgson the old drawing-master who was one of the founder-members. He is well known for his treacly oils of Norwich buildings but he exhibited other subjects, some of which are described as sketches and may have been water-colours. His life was uneventful. In 1825 he was appointed 'Painter of Domestic Architecture to H.R.H. the Duke of Sussex', but H.R.H. was rather fond of distributing these honorific appointments and it is doubtful if it implied more practical patronage. Besides helping with his father's practice and continuing it after his father's death he became drawing-master at the Norwich Grammar School. Norwich Castle holds a number of his sketchbooks, mostly architectural pencil work and a few full water-colours which at times reach considerable heights. He is clearly of the school of Crome and is a little reminiscent of Thirtle, Stark, and Churchyard but there seem to be no water-colours identifiable other than these at Norwich (Plates 53a, 53b).

So far these artists we have considered were in some degree professionals but all the time a great deal of work was being done and exhibited by amateurs. There must have been hundreds of them. Every person who pretended to a polite education in the city and its neighbourhood must at some time or other have learned to use the pencil or the brush. As early as 1784, well before the water-colouring craze was at its peak, Jaggers of Norwich thought it worth their while to advertise in the local press that they could supply a new type of water-colour in cakes.

With such masters as they had it is not surprising that the Norwich amateurs often achieved a fair level of competence and sometimes much more. The Gurney girls, Crome's pupils, occasionally show individuality. Norwich Castle contains a distinctive pencil drawing heightened with white and blue by Richenda Gurney (Mrs Cunningham) but this is dated as late as 1855; in the same collection there is a competent pencil drawing by her sister Louisa done in 1805 while she was still Crome's pupil. Another pupil of Crome whose work collectors may come across was Maria Brown, who became the wife of Henry

Hansell. Crome gave her one of his delicate monochrome wash drawings which is still in the possession of her descendants. There is a drawing by her in Norwich Castle of Hockford Church, signed and dated 1826, which shows by its style that she had also been a pupil of Cotman. The Castle also contains one water-colour well above average by a Miss Glover who seems to have been a follower of Crome and perhaps of Thirtle; it is a good picture, not a copy nor obviously derivative, and if a fair sample of her work it shows that she was better than some of the professionals. Also good at his best was Captain (later Major-General) James Pattison Cockburn (1778–1849) of the Royal Artillery, who evidently studied under Thirtle when stationed at Norwich. He first exhibited as an Honorary Member in 1809. There is one Cockburn water-colour of Norwich Cathedral at the Castle which if it were not inscribed would pass as Thirtle's work. Unfortunately Cockburn fell into the fault that bedevilled many of the earlier English water-colourists, professional and amateur alike; he sometimes made drawings that were far too big for what was in them. They are occasionally to be found and are not difficult to recognize as they have a sort of 'Cromish' breadth about them. But he did better work, much of which is probably snugly attributed to greater names. A sketch of his of *The Valley of Früdegen*, Switzerland, was engraved by James Duffield Harding in 1819. In the following year Cockburn published a volume containing sixty-two views of *Swiss Scenery*. These were not engraved by Harding but he did engrave forty-nine others by Cockburn for a book of *Views to Illustrate the Route of the Simplon* which was published in 1822. Other engravings after Cockburn appeared in W. B. Cooke's *Views in Rome*, 1840. Cockburn is a good example of that type of army officer who by long practice, persistence and skill played a creditable part in the art of the time. *The Cavalry Barracks, Norwich* (Plate 23a) has something about it of G. Fennell Robson whose work was so prominent a feature of the Old Water Colour Society's Exhibition in the twenties.

These pupils of Crome and of Thirtle generally retained some personality of their own, but the earlier pupils of Cotman seemed content to acquire as much as they could of their master's almost machine-like certitude with the pencil. They had varying success. Mrs Dawson Turner and her daughters were soon able to turn out tolerably close copies of Cotman's architectural drawings. Many of these are in the British Museum in Dawson Turner's extra-illustrated copy of Blomefield's *History of Norfolk*, and still more in the City Library at Norwich and in the Ashmolean. Altogether it is plain that Dawson Turner drove his family hard but would have been better satisfied with a good camera. Another of Cotman's pupils by whom some sufficiently distinctive water-colours survive is Ellen Day. Most of her drawings are no more than versions of Cotman and might have been done by any of his more competent pupils, but her water-colours of architectural 'bits' about the city are her own by virtue of their strong dark tones. There is no danger of them being mistaken for the work of any other Norwich artist; for which one is thankful.

But these are small fry compared with the two amateurs now to be considered, Robert Leman (1799–1863) and Thomas Lound (1802–61), who occupy a central and important position in the history of Norwich water-colours.

Robert Leman has for some reason been neglected. Dickes mentioned him only three times, once as Honorary Secretary of the Norfolk and Norwich Arts Union and twice as a member of the Norwich Amateur Club; Cundall mentions him once, among the also-rans, as an amateur. Nor is his reputation advanced by the *Conway Castle*, illustrated in G. V. Barnard's *Painters of the Norwich School*, in which the castle is softly modelled and weightless and occupies an indeterminate position in an undistinguished landscape. There were, however, thirteen water-colours in the 1927 Exhibition in his name. There is little that is amateurish about much of Leman's work, which would rank high in any company. His pencil drawings are of an even level of professional brilliance; their fault lies in their faultlessness. He exhibited first in 1819 and afterwards spasmodically and little. His water-colours, which are uncommon, show at their best decisive drawing, clear colour, and a feeling of spaciousness which gives them great distinction. In his *Snowdon from Capel Curig* he achieved one of the finest water-colours of the School (Colour Plate IV).

Leman seems to have been a pupil of John Sell Cotman. *Cattle in a Pool* (Plate 56a) with its strong Cotman-cum-Varley flavour was a considerable puzzle until the appearance of Mr Arnold Fellows *Trees* (Plate 56b) provided the link with later and more familiar Lemans. Like his master, Leman is a classic in spirit, and is perhaps the only one of Cotman's followers who genuinely appreciated and seized upon this quality in his work. Apart from this the distinctive feature of Leman's water-colours is a high colour-key in which a pale straw-yellow, pale blues, and light purples prevail. Despite the occasional similarity of Leman to Lound, to Bright, and to Middleton, I believe his distinctive manner was his own consistent development of what he had learned from Cotman, and that when the others resembled him it was because of their common heritage.

Thomas Lound is both widely known and generally admired. Born to a brewer's business, which Johnson called 'the opportunity of growing rich beyond the dreams of avarice'; he made use of the opportunity to collect pictures and to paint pictures himself. At the sale after his death in 1861 there were listed seventy-five drawings by Thirtle, twenty-two by Bright, twenty-four by Stannard, seventy-seven sketches by members of the Amateur Club, studies in crayon by Crome, a sketchbook and *A Moonlight* by J. B. Crome, four water-colours by Cotman, one by Miles Edmund Cotman, two pictures by

Plate V *Dreadnought and Grampus, Hospital Ships on the Thames* Miles Edmund Cotman (1810–1858)

Stannard, a Vincent, three by David Cox, drawings by Callow, Dibdin, and Samuel Prout, together with forty-six paintings and 307 drawings by himself.

Lound was an eclectic and there is considerable variety in his work, which, as it is seldom dated, cannot easily be grouped into periods. Cotman was his master but only a few early drawings show the relationship between his work and Cotman's famous circulating portfolios. Despite his admiration for Cotman, Crome, and Thirtle, the most evident influence in Lound's mature work was that of David Cox. One might reasonably guess that most of his Cox-like work in which the colour is built up by a number of swift (and in Lound's case often rather meaningless) touches of the brush was done in the late forties, whereas a group which recalls the work of another of Cox's pupils, William Bennett the younger, was perhaps done in the fifties and may be the last, or nearly the last, of Lound's several manners. Some of his best-known work, in particular the sepias, I believe to date from the thirties and to derive less from Cotman than from his eldest son, Miles, of whom more later; but these also show the revealing criss-cross touches which connect with Cox. But whenever they were produced, it is normal to find that Lound's drawings have been done before by somebody else; so that every Lound is, as it were, a Thirtle or a Cotman or a Bright or a Cox or a somebody else seen à la Lound. No essential Lound appears to have existed independently of others, and yet he is personal enough to stamp all these versions as his. Only in his smaller sketchbook material, which is sometimes rather good, do we seem perhaps to be getting a glimpse of the man himself. He was an unpolished, popular man and his work has an appealing masculine frankness about it. His drawing is usually good, but his colour is of varying quality; sometimes as in Mr Geoffrey Allen's *Boathouse on the Yare at Reedham* (Plate 61a) it is subtle and refined; but more often it is unhappily ambitious and his distances, particularly when mountains are involved, have a touch of the cinema organ. He first exhibited at Norwich in 1820. After Cotman and Bright he was the most prolific water-colourist of the School, and though he never reached Leman's heights he is not to be despised.

Two years Lound's senior, the professional Samuel David Colkett (1800–63) is a more individual water-colourist than has been supposed. Although his work in oils has been well known his water-colours until lately seem to have disappeared. The basis upon which we can begin to re-establish Colkett is a little rural scene painted very wetly in bright fresh colours, signed and dated 1832, in the collection of Mr Geoffrey Allen (Plate 54b). On their likeness to this we can add two others in my own collection (Plates 55a, 55b). One of these gives a clue, I believe, to the disappearance of Colkett for it was sold to me as by Thomas Churchyard (1798–1865). Now Churchyard's name is known to be rather loosely employed for a whole range of otherwise unidentified water-colours. He was an Ipswich man, had a long life, was a considerable collector, and a prolific amateur water-colourist, some of whose undated works reach a very high level indeed. Churchyard has not yet been sufficiently studied and his style is by many only vaguely conceived; he has consequently turned into a convenient receptacle for, I think, such people as Samuel Colkett and David Hodgson. I have since seen other 'Churchyards' which seemed to be by the same hand as Mr Allen's picture. Churchyard exhibited at Norwich as an Honorary Member in 1829 and 1852; at his best he was far better than a good Colkett, and at his worst never as bad as Colkett could be (Plate 54a). Colkett was a pupil of James Stark but his water-colours have something in common technically with late Cox or even Constable; which is not to say they are of remotely comparable merit.

Obadiah Short (1803–86) is not even mentioned by Dickes or Cundall but was represented in the 1927 Loan Exhibition by three oils and one water-colour (*Landscape at Costessey, Norfolk*). There is a good deal of sketchbook material by him at Norwich Castle which needs working on. He is not a great artist waiting to be discovered but a pleasant minor talent who should not be ignored. A set of twelve small drawings of Mousehold Heath in dark rich tones is quite individual and recalls no other member of the School unless it be J. S. Cotman in his 1810 manner; this, however, is unlikely to be a direct influence as Short was only 7 at the time and we should probably look rather to the example of John Varley (Plate 64a). As the only full-scale water-colour by Short that I have seen is also a 'skyline' picture of Mousehold it may be that he was predisposed to view his landscapes in this way.

The last of this group of painters is that very individual amateur the Rev. E. T. Daniell (1804–43) whose work at its best is of great distinction. He was educated at Norwich Grammar School when Crome was drawing-master there and then went on to Balliol and took a degree in 1828. He exhibited first at Norwich in 1832. Much of his leisure was spent in Joseph Stannard's studio in Norwich where he learned to etch.[1] He was less a provincial than any other member of the School, even than Cotman, for although his home was in Norwich his years at Oxford gave him wider contacts and interests. In 1825 he was already a friend and patron of John Linnel, who was the father-in-law of Samuel Palmer and a friend of William Blake. In 1829 and the following year Daniell toured France, Italy, and Switzerland, sketching in both oil and water-colour. In 1830 he visited Scotland and Ireland. In 1832 he exhibited at the Norfolk and Suffolk Society's Exhibition and at the end of that year took Holy Orders and exhibited in Norwich no more.

[1] And with whom later he had a law suit, for Stannard built a studio which obscured Daniell's light. Daniell won the case and the studio came down.

There are a number of drawings by Daniell at Norwich Castle, at the Victoria and Albert, and in the British Museum, but elsewhere they are not frequently seen (Plates 64b–66). Those that derive from the later tours are dated but the earlier drawings which contain the secret of his development up to 1829 are not. He was a fine etcher but as a water-colourist he seems to be afraid of colour. Save that his manner was free and bold he was really a tinted draughtsman closer to Francis Towne than to a pure water-colourist like Peter de Wint. And here perhaps we have found the root of Daniell's style, not in Crome the painter in oils who had been his earliest master, but in Cotman the great draughtsman whom he deeply admired.

The years from 1812 to 1824 which Cotman had spent producing antiquarian drawings and engravings in Yarmouth were the water-shed of the Norwich School. His teaching from 1807 to 1812 had borne little fruit. The older masters, Crome, Hodgson, Ladbrooke, and Thirtle had already impressed their personalities on the younger talent before Cotman's arrival. From 1805 until 1824 the Society and its exhibitions were dominated by Crome and his son but from 1824 onward until the seventies and eighties the peculiar light of John Sell Cotman's genius gave to the School both direction and stimulus.

But before we follow Cotman from Yarmouth back to Norwich we must notice a number of Yarmouth men who, though not clearly his pupils, were not unaffected by his example and who, though not necessarily exhibitors at Norwich, have a claim to be considered members of the School.

William Joy (1803–67) and John Cantiloe Joy (1806–66) were the sons of the guard on the Yarmouth to Ipswich mail coach. It is not clear whether this was the R. B. Joy who was a member of the Norwich Society in 1808–10 and who gave his address as 'at Mr R. Ladbrooke's'. He exhibited a portrait, an historical-dramatic subject, and *A Boy looking at a Bird*. William and John Cantiloe were born in Yarmouth and were fortunate to attract the attention of Captain G. W. Manby, the barrack-master at Yarmouth, who achieved fame by his invention of a mortar for firing life-lines to wrecks. It was Manby who is said to have directed their art to the sea (did Yarmouth artists need such direction?) and to have employed them as well as others to show the horrors of shipwreck in order to publicize his life-saving devices. William exhibited at the Norwich Society in 1814 and later in 1823 and again in 1828. In 1832 they removed to Portsmouth where the Government employed them to record the various craft used in the fishing trade. Afterwards they moved to London, then to Chichester, then to Putney, and finally back to London. They are commonly said to have worked together so that their pictures are the work of 'the brothers Joy' (Plate 52a). Although often true they had distinct manners and in their earlier work there is little difficulty in ascribing to each his share. William was the broader and livelier painter and was generally responsible for boisterous green seas and storm-swept skies: John Cantiloe was more clearly of the line of the Cleveleys and the Dutch painters of mirror-like calms: in their combined works it was probably he who supplied the detail. In the pictures which they made separately a difference of palette is at once evident, William showing a preference for heavier tones, for seas of almost seaweed-green, skies of middle grey, and a peculiar shade of pea-green which he used often on his ships; whereas his brother's palette was higher in key, more varied, and with a leaning towards browns and blues. Their later pictures I find less attractive; the colours are heightened to give meretricious appeal: white sails and blue seas have to be *very* good to step out of the throng of such things. Although they are thought of as marine painters only there are a number of monochrome landscape sketches by them in the Yarmouth Library. They are not good. The Joys are said to have been self-taught but the evidence already given suggests a father taught by Robert Ladbrooke and the influence of Cotman is apparent in Williams' work. A water-colour in my own collection changed hands several times as a Miles Edmund Cotman before its true author became apparent.

The Joys are known and their works sought after, but another Yarmouth artist of very real merit is nowadays little heard of. This is William Howes Hunt (1806–79) who suffers from the disadvantage of having the same initials as three other artists of his name.[1] He began as a draper but turned professional artist. Hunt engraved some views of Yarmouth and etched 'after Rembrandt'. An etching of St Benet's Abbey by him both drawn and etched in 1831, which is in the British Museum, has a pencilled note on it, 'Drawing in Collection of J.R.': this is a sepia monochrome, one of several which reached the British Museum with the Reeve Collection. These monochromes are of real quality, keenly felt, firmly and sensitively drawn, and have that typically Dutch air of pellucid calm. Of his water-colours I have so far found few. That in Yarmouth Library (Plate 67a) by its mellow colour and modest drawing makes one anxious to see more. A very similar picture in Norwich Castle attributed to Hunt is probably the work of Lound, unless Hunt himself caught the rather hard and slashing brush technique which derived from Bright. That Hunt enjoyed a reputation among his friends is evident, for he not only engraved his own work but other engravings were made after it by Richard Girling.

The Girling brothers, Edmund (1796–1871) and Richard (1799–1863), were no doubt principally engravers. Edmund etched in the manners of Rembrandt and Waterloo. Richard on the other hand engraved several pictures after Crome, after the brothers Joy, after William Howes Hunt, and after his own sketches. I am inclined to think that they were of Yarmouth; Edmund was certainly a bank-clerk there. Richard spent some years

[1] William Holman Hunt, William Henry Hunt, William Harvey Hunt.

in London. Their water-colouring achievement seems so far to be limited to one landscape of Cumberland in Norwich Castle (Plate 41b) which is inscribed 'Girling' on the back. It is no doubt by one of the brothers but until more work by them appears it is impossible to say which. It has a breadth and strength which suggests that they were followers of Crome.

If the Society to which Cotman returned in 1824 was much changed so was he. The years of concentration upon drawing and engraving medieval architecture had emphasized the linear nature of his art: for a while he had been a draughtsman rather than a painter. In colour he had passed from his blue period, through the exquisite greens and browns of the Yorkshire drawings, to the deep mulberry-browns and rich splashes of colour with which he made his water-colours as powerful as oils. Then for some years he had abandoned colour altogether, only to resume it in a new and occasionally startling manner. In *The Needles* (*c.* 1817) (Kitson, Plate 88) there are, though with a difference such as Richter would have approved, the clear light washes essentially 'of the medium' such as he had used in 1805; but in *Mont St Michel* (Kitson, Plate 111) he recurs to the chromatic violence of 1810, though now instead of rich deep colour and stormy tonal contrast he relies upon the brilliance of golden-yellows and azure-blues to recall the sun-drenched summer days of Normandy. But in general, as he emerged from his labour of drawing churches and produced work that gave delight instead of information, Cotman used sepia and not colour. It was the Master of *Landscape near Domfront* (Kitson, Plate 98) and *Castle of Mortain* (Kitson, Plate 100) who taught for a critical few years the younger generation of Norwich artists—not the Master of *Greta Bridge* (Oppé, Plate VIII).

The nine years of Cotman's second Norwich period show him trying to adjust his style, not in accordance with the natural development forced on him by his own temperament, but in an effort to hit the taste of the public. This seems to have begun before he left Yarmouth. In 1822 he fell into a fit of depression so deep that he and his family firmly believed that he was dying. It happened that John Varley was visiting Dawson Turner; he forced his way into Cotman's bedroom and assured the patient that according to his astrological predictions he was not to die for at least ten years. A number of Varley's own works are attributable to this Norfolk visit and it is probable that he was there for some time. He had contributed two landscapes to the Norwich Exhibition in 1809, a *View of Wales* and *Landscape—Evening* and now in 1823 he became an Honorary Member of the Society and sent four more drawings. Over the next two or three years several of Cotman's water-colours seem to be reaching out for popular approval by emulating Varley. The results were not much like Varley but they mark a new type of Cotman. To the years 1822 to 1826 can be attributed a distinctive group of water-colours of fine quality. They are rare and because more free from individual mannerism than others of his drawings are not always easily recognized. In them Cotman aims at and achieves a greater degree of naturalism than usual; they are marked by a less austere simplification of form, greater attention to modelling and to atmospheric perspective, by gentler skies, by noticeable use of soft pale blue and russet and, most conspicuously of all, by the use of the razor for scratching out lights and for texturing his paper—a technique he employed neither much before nor much after this date.[1] The splendid *Snowdon with the Lake of Llanberis, near Dolbadern Castle, North Wales* (Plate 36b) from the Bulwer Collection and now in the possession of Lord Mackintosh, one of the largest of his drawings, was exhibited in Norwich in 1824 but was based on a sketch made on his Welsh tour in 1802. The difference of his approach at this time is well shown by a comparison between *Mills at Crowland* (Plate 37a) and *A Draining Mill* (Plate 37b) *c.* 1831, two of several drawings which he developed from a sketch taken in 1804. Although all the naturalistic drawings of this period seem to be studio work recapturing scenes visited in earlier days, they have a freshness which arises perhaps from his joy in relinquishing antiquarian work and resuming picture-making in a manner, novel to him because more conventional, which challenged his full powers.

Dawson Turner wrote to him in June 1826 in reply to one of Cotman's despairing letters—'You have lived long enough to learn that your present style will not succeed, and you have talent enough to adopt any other. The public is a body that cannot be forced. Some extraordinary geniuses may have succeeded in guiding it; but they are few, and the great part of those who have made the experiment have failed. Such amongst us who have to live by it must be content to follow its taste.' This is the echo of what Francis Cholmeley had written concerning Cotman's lack of success twenty years before—'. . . if any defects in your Stile of Drawing have a share in causing it, you will have *Will and Perseverance*, as you certainly have *Power* to correct these faults'.

The year in which Dawson Turner's letter was written was for Cotman yet another of black despair—'The sun has set for ever on my career and all is darkness before me.' It was one of the deepest and most prolonged of his attacks of melancholia and while it lasted he produced nothing. Towards the autumn of that year he began to rouse himself and the direction of his thoughts is shown in another letter to Dawson Turner—'I can no longer bear the stigma that Trees I can neither draw nor paint.'

His remaining years in Norwich, save for the recurrent periods of misery, were fully employed. The depression of the national economy which had reduced drawing pupils from a flood to a trickle gave place to prosperity, and in 1827 Hudson Gurney wrote to

[1] It is, however, found occasionally in his early work of the London period.

Dawson Turner that Cotman was getting on very well as a drawing-master, and that if he persisted he would have all the business that was available in Norwich because John Berney Crome was losing his pupils rapidly. Necessary though such work might be to maintain his family the social status of drawing-master was not what Cotman had looked for, nor did it give him time to produce as much original work as he wished. Nevertheless, as usual with Cotman, a great deal was done. The production of these years was of three kinds: first, drawings to serve as copies for his pupils; second, the most sustained body of work in oils which he ever achieved; and third, occasional water-colours for exhibition both at Norwich and at the Water Colour Society in London.[1] Behind much of this work, though not all, there is evidence of a determined but not altogether successful attempt to eliminate the idiosyncracies of his style and to produce work comprehensible to the public. The criticism that he could neither draw nor paint trees was met by a group of fine oils which, while they demonstrate to us that he could do so with genius, were so unlike any other painter's representation of trees that his contemporaries remained unenthusiastic. This attempt in oils was paralleled by a similar effort in water-colour, so that the 'enchanted bath-sponge' convention of the Yorkshire drawings was now fairly consistently replaced by a convention which he had used sporadically before, best described as the 'banana-hand method', a convention which Varley shared. Combined with this change he also in his landscapes tried to use a colour range less personal and more to the public's taste. That it met with some success is shown by his letter to Dawson Turner in 1827 '. . . my pupils increase with a prospect of more; the heresy of a certain style is certainly losing ground'. The drawings made at this time developed out of the 'scratched' drawings of 1824 and, though perhaps the commonest, are for a reason we shall touch on presently, among the least known.

At about this time he also began to exploit another manner which seems to have antagonized the public then quite as much as it does now. In November 1828 he wrote to Dawson Turner: 'City and Town scenery and splendid architecture, mixed up with elegant scenery, make up the compositions of the day.' This was the line followed so successfully by David Roberts, J. D. Harding, and many others, in the *Landscape Annuals* but along which Cotman, tied at home by his teaching and perhaps by his wife, could only work at second-hand. Apart from his Normandy drawings all foreign subjects by Cotman derive from the sketches of others, of the Rev. James Bulwer, W. H. Harriot, Joseph Geldart, and Captain R. Elliot. As usual the drawing is done with that majestic deliberation which marks all Cotman's middle period pencil work, but it rarely conveys the immediacy of

[1] The Norwich Society was dissolved in 1825 for lack of premises but was revived in 1828 as The Norfolk and Suffolk Institute for the Promotion of Fine Arts.

first-hand observation. The colouring, brilliant yellows and blues stung by spots of emerald and scarlet, adds nothing of the romantic softness to his scenes which served J. M. W. Turner, William Havell, George Fennel Robson, and George Barret so well with a sentimental generation. Presumably, as replicas exist, some of his more startling Normandy drawings met a market. There are at least four versions of both *Mont St. Michel* and *The Abbatial House of St. Ouen at Rouen*, in spite of the criticism of the latter when it was shown in 1831—'as the greatest outrage Taste has suffered for some time, and that is saying a bold thing' (Plate 36a). Only rarely can one do more than admire these drawings but the few pictures that move more deeply such as *On the Rampart, Domfront* (Oppé, XIV) in Sir Edmund Bacon's collection, are the clue to the vision which Cotman by a formula sought to recapture. Yet if the owners of these rather gaudy pictures would close-frame and hang them with their peculiar qualities in mind instead of giving them whatever water-colour mount is fashionable at the moment I suspect we should all find ourselves more sympathetic to these brilliant drawings than we usually are.

The variations in Cotman's style had a very real effect on those who learned from him. If the sepia drawings of the early twenties are the source of E. T. Daniell's work, then Cotman's own son Miles Edmund (1810–58), six years younger than Daniell, naturally absorbed the aims which Cotman had set himself in the autumn of 1826. So it is, that of all those who depend from Cotman, his eldest son most nearly approaches what many people would call normal vision. Miles, who was always intended for his father's profession, became his principal assistant and constant supporter. For eighteen years he worked indefatigably both as a teacher and a manufacturer of drawing copies.[1] So closely did they collaborate in this manufacture that the father unhesitatingly put his name to his son's work and even presented it as his own. Sometimes, if his mood did not allow him to produce a drawing for the Water Colour Society Exhibition, Miles would do one for him so that his Associateship should not lapse, to which he would add little but the signature. Naturally many drawings of this period cannot with certainty be attributed to Miles or to his father. Some of Miles's work is easy to identify; it is usually attractive, occasionally brilliant, but sometimes a shade tight or, as his father said, 'hard' in its handling: it is, in my view, rather pedestrian (Plates 69a, 69b, 70a). The greater number of the drawings which it is traditional to doubt suggest, if we are to account for them, a greater variation in Miles's work than we have evidence for, or else that John Sell had a hand in them. The suggestion (*Walker's Quarterly 21*) that Miles Cotman's work is chameleon-like and might, if not signed, be attributed to such names as Varley, Cox, Müller or Bonington is misleading. In so far as there is a resemblance, it is not due to

[1] Their great library eventually consisted of over 4,000 drawings.

Plate VI *A Barn* Henry Bright (1810–1873)

Miles Edmund's imitating them but to their common debt to his father. Müller certainly can be like Miles Cotman, but here the admiration of Müller for John Sell and Müller's association with James Bulwer make it clear which way the influence went. It is customary for some people to pronounce that all the more conventional Cotman family drawings are by Miles, but experts gain more in repute by denying than affirming, and it simply will not do to assume that Cotman himself, when he was proclaimedly trying to do more conventional drawings, did not do some at least of these. But perhaps who did them is not very material, for though they are often good and never bad, they are rarely, I think, great.

But Cotman, industrious, prolific, and emotionally fully committed to his art, could not have maintained an unchanging style even had he hit upon a vein of ore. While these more conventional water-colours were being done the natural development inevitable in the style of a still-vital artist was taking place and a new and turbulent note began to appear. This is the quality which was seized on by another of his pupils, the son of a lawyer, Joseph Geldart (1808–82). Geldart has little justification for appearing here at all because although a good draughtsman in charcoal and wash, I can find no evidence that he ever used colour—which is strange, for he is said to have spent some years of his life trying to discover the colour secrets of the Venetian painters (Plates 68a, 68b). He became Cotman's pupil in 1829 and showed him a sketch he had made in Switzerland of the Via Mala. From this sketch Cotman made the great drawing now in Norwich Castle, of which Geldart wrote that it 'has a double interest for me in the fact that, at my first lesson, it was made before me by J. S. Cotman from a very slight and imperfect sketch made by me the year before; and also because the Master was at the time suffering from one of those fits of deep melancholy to which he was periodically subject, and which rendered it almost impossible for him to speak or even to look up' (Plate 39a).

This drawing may mark a turning-point in Cotman's further development for it was soon afterwards that he began to use fermented flour-paste, a medium on which he based one of his finest groups of water-colours. The first dated example, 1830, in this medium is *Middleton Tower, Norfolk* (Cundall, Plate XLIII) and from then on the jewelled richness and depth of colour peculiar to this method frequently appear. Many things contributed to Cotman's adoption of it. He had learned, as had many other water-colourists towards the middle of the century, to enjoy the depth and richness that could be obtained with oil-painting. But the materials for oil-painting were expensive and sale for his work was doubtful; by means of his flour-paste he was able to obtain much of the effect of oil at less expense. It is also possible that Cotman felt himself hampered by the extent of his control over water-colour. Whereas most who have used the medium have found some delight in seizing upon its fortuitous effects, one cannot feel that with Cotman there ever were fortuitous effects, and those accidental irregularities which can add so much are normally absent from his drawings. But the paste medium was essentially a medium of inequality and the accidental tonal discrepancies which in pure water-colour he would have had to contrive in deliberate fashion now flowed richly from his brush. There is a greater immediacy in this work than there had been for some time, a more direct translation of his ideas into visual terms.

The most famous of these early flour-paste drawings is *Storm on Yarmouth Beach* (Plate 38a) now at Norwich Castle, in which a portentous storm-cloud rolls above a group of fishermen working with their nets. In this drawing Cotman also employs another device which is characteristic of his work of the early thirties although it had appeared as early as 1824, that of edging principal features with a sepia brush line.

As Cotman's eldest son naturally learned and absorbed the manner that was current with his father from 1824–28 when he was at the most impressionable age, so the work of his second son, John Joseph (1814–78), was rooted in his father's mood of 1828–34. It was not at first intended that J. J. Cotman should become an artist but his youthful experience in his uncle's shop confirmed his disinclination to commerce, and like Miles Edmund he joined his father's 'factory'. There are two water-colours in Mr E. Hinde's collection which show a calmness of spirit untypical of most of his mature work and indeed untypical of what we know of his character at any age, but which probably date from his 'teens.

John Sell Cotman's recurrent bouts of despair were a mental malady which he transmitted in varying degree to his children. His eldest son, Miles, became no worse than a slightly eccentric melancholic; his daughter, Anne, said of herself: 'I am a strange girl . . . whom it would puzzle a conjuror to make out'; John Joseph developed so intense an excitability that he was confined at his family's instance for a short time in 1837, and throughout his life showed a far more than average mental instability; Walter was almost unemployable; Alfred, the youngest, became violently insane and entered an asylum in 1841. During Cotman's second Norwich period these miserable developments were in the future, but John Sell himself was unable to combat the agonies of his own temperament and sometimes month after month went by during which he could barely raise his head and each day seemed to him an endless misery. In 1828, for example, no work of his is known and from this prolific letter-writer not a letter exists dated to that year. In 1833 the Turner family again came to the rescue by putting him on the scent of an appointment as Professor of Drawing at the newly-founded King's College at London. To gain this appointment Cotman roused himself, went up to London, and canvassed intensively.

He was successful, and at first the post seemed to give him many of the things he most desired and needed: a position of some dignity, a residence in London, 'the only place for an artist to breathe in' (as he himself wrote to John Joseph) and, though not affluence, a greater measure of security.

Once again it was a move of Cotman's which marked a period in the development of the Norwich School.

5

The Persisting Tradition

THE NORWICH SOCIETY had passed through some difficult times. The secessionist exhibitions of Ladbrooke and his associates in 1816 did little serious harm and lasted only three years, but in 1825 the Society lost its exhibition rooms and ceased to exist. Three years later it was re-formed as The Norfolk and Suffolk Institution for the Promotion of Fine Arts. Under this title it held six more annual exhibitions until 1833 when, with Cotman's removal to London, it lost its mainspring and dissolved.[1] But the existence of the Norwich School did not depend upon a formal organization. According to a circular of 1828, although the Society had by that time exhibited 4,600 pictures, scarcely one had been sold in its rooms and the receipts at the door had never covered expenses. This was strangely at variance with the experience of other provincial cities which had followed Norwich's example in holding annual exhibitions. The Leeds Society in 1823 took at the door more than £600 and sold pictures to the value of £1,340. Carlisle and Newcastle had done as well in proportion; while at the first Royal Manchester Exhibition J. B. Crome had sold a picture, David Hodgson two, and James Stark five.

The body of artists who had composed the Society continued to be active after its dissolution. Of the original members although John Ninham, Crome and Dixon were dead, Robert Ladbrooke and John Thirtle were still working.

Ladbrooke, a difficult unamiable man, had become something of a solitary and after the failure of his secessionist group took no part in collective activities until 1824, when in response to a not very gracious olive branch from the President, John Berney Crome, he sent one or two pictures to the exhibitions. In 1822 he seems to have relinquished his teaching practice to his sons and from then on managed, presumably, to live on the

---

[1] It made repeated reappearances under several titles. 'The Norfolk and Norwich Art Union' held its first exhibition in 1839: the 'Norwich Polytechnic' its first exhibition in 1840: 'The East of England Art Union' its first exhibition in 1842: 'The Norfolk and Norwich Association for Promotion of Fine Arts Exhibition' in 1848 . . . and so on.

earnings from his pictures. From 1821 to 1832 he worked on a project to illustrate the Churches of Norfolk with some 700 drawings lithographed by his son. Of this publication Dickes wrote 'the views are ordinary, the lithography indifferent and the printing execrable'.

John Thirtle, from the firm base of his picture-framing business, continued to produce his quiet-toned pictures of the reaches of the River Yare in a manner nearer to the sketches of de Wint than to anyone expressly of Norwich. He seems to have been immune to the feverish search for higher colour, and to the fashion for drawing on coloured papers, which became general throughout England in the late twenties and the thirties. Thirtle's drawings are usually undated and undateable, but some which are evidently late show a freer and stronger manner than usual (Plates 19b, 20).

Of the middle group of Norwich men, David Hodgson continued his uneventful life as a drawing-master at Norwich Grammar School, steadily producing rather fat oils of picturesque architectural corners of the city to which his surviving water-colour sketches are subordinate. Joseph Stannard died in 1830. George Vincent, whose life is thought to have ended disastrously in 1831, was beginning to emerge as a water-colourist with an individual manner. John Berney Crome lived indeed until 1842 but his later years were clouded. Soon after Cotman's return to Norwich he began to lose his pupils. A grand manner, a lavish style of living, and a partiality to port, ended in bankruptcy in 1831. Sometime after 1833 he moved to Yarmouth where by teaching and painting 'Moonlights' he subsisted until his death. James Stark, though always 'Stark of Norwich' left for London in 1830 but continued from time to time to exhibit in his native city.

Of the remaining artists of the middle period, John Berney Ladbrooke, Henry Ninham, Thomas Lound, and Samuel David Colkett, continued to provide a hard core of those to whom Crome had been a starting-point, although Lound was now beginning to receive influences from beyond the School. The Cotman tradition was upheld by others.

When John Sell Cotman moved to London to become Professor of Drawing at King's College he left behind him at Norwich his son, Miles Edmund, as heir to the teaching practice, and took with him to London as his *aide* his second son, John Joseph. Upon these two much of the future of the Norwich School depended.

There are four artists worth mention who derive from Miles Edmund Cotman. The first is Alfred Priest (1810–50) known chiefly, although not greatly esteemed, as a painter of oils. He had been a pupil of Henry Ninham and later of Stark. I have seen only two water-colours certainly by him, both in Norwich Castle. They are best described as clumsy romanticized 'Miles Edmunds' lit by a slightly unexpected cinema-organ sky (Plate 67b). They are without discernible merit.

Far more common are the water-colours of John Sell Cotman's friend and pupil the

Reverend James Bulwer (1794–1879). Born at Norwich, Bulwer was at Jesus College, Cambridge, where in 1818 he took his degree and Orders the same year. He was first a curate in Ireland and then travelled for two years in Portugal and Madeira. A curacy at St Mary Redcliffe, Bristol, was followed by preferment in London in 1833. In 1840 he returned to Norfolk as curate of Blickling and Aylsham; in 1848 he became Vicar of Hunworth-cum-Stody where he remained until his death in 1879. It is clear from this catalogue of his movements that if he was in fact Cotman's pupil it must have been in his 'teens, because by 1812 Cotman had left for Yarmouth and soon afterwards Bulwer was in Cambridge.[1] Further contact between them was improbable until 1834 when both were living in London.

Bulwer was at heart an antiquarian. Whilst in Somerset he collected material to illustrate Collinson's *History of Somerset* and spent the latter part of his life doing the same for Blomefield's *History of Norfolk*. Many of the illustrations he did himself but a considerable number were by Miles Edmund Cotman, who at one time worked for him at half a guinea a drawing. Bulwer's own work consists chiefly of competent topographical drawings in Miles Cotman's manner, but the impression that they are good is soon dispelled if a genuine Miles Edmund gets among them. Despite the firm, rather over-decisive drawing, the strongly contrasted tones and the solid colours, James Bulwer's water-colours somehow give an impression of slightness, almost of flimsiness. A very distinctive characteristic is a tendency to over-narrow and tall church towers. His drawings have more of landscape and atmosphere about them than those of the older school of topographers but they are usually subordinated to his antiquarian purpose (Plate 47b). Pure landscapes by him are not common but do exist; two in the British Museum have an unusual quality of airiness, and another at Norwich dates from his Bristol curacy (Plate 47a). Among the best are a group in the National Gallery, Washington, which derive from the collection of his grandson, Henry Bulwer of British Columbia. Another unusual departure for Bulwer is a drawing at present with the Leger Gallery of the ceremonial opening of Clifton Suspension Bridge with many red-coats in attendance. I have seen some pure landscapes which are from quite late in his life; his style altered little.

The greater part of Bulwer's collection of Norfolk material is now in Norwich Castle where the names of Frederick Sandys, C. J. Winter, and James Bulwer seem to have been put indiscriminately to a great series of water-colours of Norfolk churches that reveal very little stylistic difference. A good many drawings of purely antiquarian interest, records of brasses and stained windows, are attributed to Sandys, probably correctly. But whether, as has been assumed, this is that Anthony Frederick Augustus Sandys who

[1] The Rev. A. Bulwer was subscriber to Cotman's *Architectural Antiquities of Norfolk* in 1812.

came within the Pre-Raphaelite Circle is far less likely. This Sandys was born at Norwich in 1832 and exhibited a portrait at the Royal Academy before he was 20. If he is the man responsible for the drawings in the Bulwer Collection they are probably juvenilia but it is more likely that the antiquarian Sandys was a relation.

But Miles Edmund Cotman, who inherited half of his father's skill and genius, though himself an admirable water-colourist, was not a fruitful influence. The future of what was good in the School derived from the other half of John Sell Cotman's personality, from the demonic visionary of *Storm on Yarmouth Beach*—from the half inherited by his second son, John Joseph (Colour Plate VII).

The arrangement that John Joseph should help his father in London was not successful. The patient, self-sacrificing Miles was better suited to the trying task of living out the hurricanes of his father's enthusiasms and enduring the misery of his semi-conscious months of depression. An exchange was made in 1834, and John Joseph returned to Norwich where he struggled to maintain the teaching practice. But the emotional strain was too great, and for some months in 1837 it became necessary to confine him in a mental home while Miles returned to Norwich to keep the practice together until his brother recovered.

At this time another star of more than average brilliance appeared in the person of Henry Bright (1810–73). He was born at Saxmundham in Suffolk in the same year as Miles Edmund Cotman and four years earlier than John Joseph, but is more decidedly of the new age than either. He started his career as a chemist's assistant first at Woodbridge and eventually at Norwich. As his master, Paul Squire, was a collector of pictures Bright naturally came into contact with the Norwich artists and amongst them discovered his vocation. He gave up the chemist's trade and his indentures were transferred to Alfred Stannard[1] under whom the remainder of his apprenticeship was spent. He also took lessons from John Sell Cotman and John Berney Crome. In 1836 he moved to London and in 1839 became a Member of the New Society of Painters in Water-Colour.

Bright was an original artist. He was a draughtsman of superlative competence and a technical innovator without equal. Although a prolific worker his pure water-colours are comparatively rare and not always easy to recognize as they usually pre-date his distinctive later manners. Bright developed his typical style from the basis of the reinforced black chalk and the brilliant dark-toned paste drawings which John Sell Cotman was doing in the mid-thirties, and came so to mix his media that one regards a Bright drawing as a unique hybrid in which water-colour, body-colour, gummed shadows, charcoal, and pastel are indiscriminately used. The result of this *mélange* is almost invariably brilliant, almost

[1] Of whom as a water-colourist we as yet know nothing.

dazzling, but at his worst his pictures are like large over-glossed, over-coloured Victorian photographic postcards. He travelled widely in Wales, Scotland, the Rhineland, and on the French coast, and his subjects latterly became those a Victorian professional photographer might choose; in fact their style may well have been based on his. He was professionally successful, but did not continue his membership of the New Society of Painters in Water-Colour for more than five years, which suggests that he later concentrated on oil or pastel. Few other artists but J. M. W. Turner made such a good thing out of art as did Bright: his income was said to have exceeded £2,000 from teaching alone.

It is fortunate that Bright commonly signed and frequently dated his work for otherwise we should be likely to draw wrong conclusions on stylistic grounds. Early dates are the less common and the black-and-white chalk drawings, which were probably done between 1828 and 1840 when the medium was in vogue, are not usually dated at all. Mr Harold Day has a beach scene in full water-colour dated 1837 which shows the contemporary enthusiasm for work of that kind by Bonington. It is an effective but a strangely faltering bit of work; perhaps such slight atmospheric pieces gave too little scope for his sense of breadth and his magnificent draughtsmanship. *Low Tide*, at the Victoria and Albert (Plate 72a), dated 1841, is a more assured attempt in the same manner. His experiment with mixed techniques began early. A gouache, pastel and water-colour drawing of a watermill in my own collection is dated 1841. It is broadly conceived, well drawn, and effective in an unusual way although, as sometimes happens with Bright, some people are moved to fury at the sight of it. There are certainly traces in it of that excess of virtuosity which later became so painful (Plate 73a). But Bright's progress away from pure water-colour was not consistent; his *Old Barn, Kent of 1847* in Norwich Castle is carried out in clear broad washes with absolute mastery of his medium; and a wholly delightful *Windmill by a River* (Plate 72b) dated 1851, is broadly conceived and broadly painted on a coarse biscuit-coloured paper similar to Cox's Scottish wrapping paper on which the whites alone, necessarily, are in body-colour. Unfortunately the more dramatically coloured works of Bright are generally unsigned and undated and we can only guess their date. I am inclined to think that the chromatic violence of such things as *Sunset at Low Tide* in the British Museum (Plate 71b) and a very dramatic *Ruined Castle on a Moonlit Crag* in my own collection are from the thirties, but they may well be twenty years later.

To a modern eye Bright's work done before manipulative efficiency overwhelmed his taste is the more attractive, but his fully-developed personal style has admirers; and although admiration is not often extended to his large exhibition pieces the same could be said of almost any mid-nineteenth-century water-colourist. Bright, though always

Plate VII *River Landscape* John Joseph Cotman (1814–1878)

reckoned a leading member of the School, spent much of his working life in London as Stark did, and rarely exhibited in Norwich. His influence appears nevertheless in the later drawings of Leman and, most clearly, in the work of Middleton.

In the meantime John Sell Cotman was expending most of his energy on the duties of Professor of Drawing at King's College. As he wrote in 1835: 'Edmund, Ann, Alfred and I are all drawing mad: Ann and Alfred working for the College pupils, with great effect in every way. They have done crack subjects, and they take wonderfully. Little do they ken by whom they are done when given under my name.' Many of these drawings are marked with a rubber stamp: COTMAN, KING'S COLLEGE, LONDON and are numbered and signed in pencil.[1] Despite all this industry in making drawing copies for the College he also found time to produce some work for sale or exhibition. Unfortunately the constant criticisms of his style had to some extent destroyed his judgement. From 1824, when he returned to Norwich and set about producing drawings calculated to give him popular fame, he had become liable to extraordinary aberrations of taste, particularly it seems during the years 1832 and 1833 and again in 1838.

It was about 1832 that he produced the most extreme examples of those drawings which are coloured almost exclusively in smalt blue and gold. Once the unusual convention has been accepted one can see that some of these are fine achievements, but in others the colour is meaningless, contributing nothing to the total effect of the drawing and, in some strange way failing in itself to communicate sensuous delight. After the lovely *Ramparts of Domfront* in Sir Edmund Bacon's collection, where the colours are muted to those of a golden evening, the best of them are perhaps the various versions of *Mont St Michel* in which the strangeness of the subject is heightened by the golden light which floods it. Less attractive to our eyes than even the most garish of his blue and gold drawings is an oddity at Norwich Castle entitled: *The Interior of Spruggins Hall, Manor of Dulfuddle, Bedfordshire, leading to the Picture Gallery: Arms of Spruggins, Gull, Whittington, Bagnigge, Kiltwaddle and Sucklethumbkins, over the doorway—vide Spruggins Gallery*. When in high spirits, as he often was, Cotman could gambol delightfully in his correspondence but he could not achieve humour in his pictures. Nor was he better suited to another vein he explored, that of the 'School of Chivalry' which had been profitable to Nash, to Cattermole, and to Bonington and which was developed later by one of Cotman's own pupils, Dante Gabriel Rossetti. He exhibited two drawings of this kind in London in 1833, one of which staggered under the title: *King John and Prince Henry at Swineshead Abbey, attended by the Earls of Salisbury, Oxford, Pembroke, Essex and Warenne; after*

[1] According to Kitson the highest known number is 4139.

their defeat and loss at crossing the Lynn Wash. Sometimes he even invented his historical occasions. In a letter to his son, Francis Walter, in 1838, he wrote: 'One entirely my own in every sense of the word, being very gay and gawdy and full of frippery, is a view on the top of Flixton Hall, Suffolk, sketched when Ann was with me some six years ago and somewhat better, with about twenty large figures, very principal, and about the same number of supernumeries or figurantes, as we say at the opera. The Story—The Presentation of a Rose and Sword to the Lady of the Manor of Flixton—a story altogether fictitious. A huge banner of Henry VIII waving over the battlements. . . . A fine subject and promises to be a very fine drawing, if so it will be 60 guineas' (Dickes, page 395). Still more odd was *Lee Shore, with the wreck of the Houghton Pictures, Books etc. sold to the Empress Catherine of Russia, including the celebrated and gorgeous Landscape of the Waggoner, by Rubens* (Kitson, 134). This was the largest, and according to himself the best drawing he ever made, 2 ft 3 in by 3 ft . . . 'which I consider for us a "Whacker" if you know what that there is, and if you do not—God help your stupidity—for a whacker it is'. The Houghton Collection was not wrecked on its way to Russia but the fiction enabled Cotman to paint in the foreground of a Miles Cotman seascape, among a tangle of dead bodies, a clutter of objects of art and *vertu*.

The Wreck of the Houghton Pictures was not the only time Cotman forced *objets d'art* into a picture. A heap of such treasures fascinated him. He was a more avid collector and frequenter of sales even than Crome. He called collecting his 'consuming passion', his 'hobby horse' and, had his income allowed him to indulge it even moderately, he might have been among the great collectors of a period rich in them. As it was he bought greedily and variously so that his Norwich home was a museum of objects; it contained not only many paintings, drawings, some 5,000 prints and 1,000 books, but armour, carvings, casts, models of ships, and curios of all kinds. In 1834 he was forced to sell his collection, and when his family was reunited with him in London and he had a home again the old passion broke out as fiercely as before.

At about this time he tried his hand again at romantic classical landscapes, inspired no doubt by the success of Barrett. They have few admirers. This, perhaps, is because his reclining nymphs, like many of the building stones of Prout, seem to be made out of half-filled feather-bolsters (Plate 38b). Yet the landscapes in which these pale beetle-grubs dance or linger are coloured with an unusual touch of mystery; though that is a poor substitute for the inspired washes of his first effort in this direction (Plate 31b).

If this sort of thing were all of Cotman at this period it would be a sad story, yet not the first time that genius has maundered into foolishness by working an unsuitable field. But one of the remarkable aspects of John Sell Cotman is the way in which again and again his pictorial sense threw up wonderful drawings in a manner quite new. The glory of the years 1834 to 1839 was not *The Houghton Pictures* nor *Flixton Hall* but that small group of brilliant little landscapes painted in his paste medium, rich, often dark in tone, simple in construction, intensely original, and equalled in achievement only by the 'Greta' drawings. These landscapes have not been dated with certainty but they probably depend from an unrecorded visit to Dartmoor made in 1835, and if so come before his more eccentric attempts to attract attention. Despite immense technical resources and an excellent visual memory Cotman's work usually lacked the breath of genius when it became too far removed from first-hand experience.[1] The best of Cotman always has the air of being done in the face of nature or at a short remove from it, and such deeply-felt landscapes as *The Shepherd* or Sir Edmund Bacon's *Mountain Scene* were not bred in London though they were certainly painted there.[2] Although they are technically water-colours these Dartmoor landscapes are really substitutes for oils; they are a sort of bastard art form such as we often meet in the work of Henry Bright. No subsequent water-colour work directly depends from them although there is a kinship of spirit between them and such later water-colours of David Cox as the *Beeston Castle* group.[3]

Contemporary with these flour-paste pictures much was done in a more conventional technique, work that showed none of the unbalance of *The Houghton Pictures*. These were chiefly marine paintings that were the product of brilliant days spent boating with his sons in the estuary of the Medway and the Thames. He wrote to his son Walter in September 1838: 'It seems that all my letters relate to my voyages up and down the Thames breathing health and spirits. To-day I took Alfred with me to Woolwich. It was such a glorious day, such clouds, such forms and colouring. I was quite beside myself and everything appeared animated. This prosperous London and its environs to me is every-thing—specially the Thames. Steamers in shoals cutting their rapid flight amid ships of all nations. In short the whole day has been one of stupendous splendour. I think I never recollect such a day as it has been.' Earlier he had made similar trips with John Joseph and with Miles Edmund, and to disentangle their hands is now always possible; although in general there is a breadth and inevitability about the organization of his drawings which Miles could not achieve.

---

[1] Kitson took a different view. Although he praised them highly he called them capriccios and dated them to 1839. A pencil drawing of the bridge at Lynmouth dated 7 August 1835 was sold at Sotheby's on 7 March 1934 and a number of chalk drawings of Dartmoor are in the British Museum. In my view these are the source of the best of the paste landscapes.
[2] Oppé, Plates XXI, XXIII.
[3] Once again it is really to Girtin's *Wharfe* drawings we must go to find anything at all comparable in simple power.

By 1839 Cotman was working chiefly in oils: in July of that year he wrote to his friend James Bulwer: 'I have been, and am, painting hard; and I am so fond of it that I think I shall never execute another drawing.' It is therefore to the later oils and to the sketches made with them in mind that one must look for the developments of this period.

But the time left for further development was short. By the autumn of 1839 the cloud which almost annually came over his mind descended again and did not lift until the summer of 1841. Then, as though in a spirit of farewell, Cotman renewed contact with his earlier life. He corresponded again with Dawson Turner after a breach of four and a half years. In September he wrote: 'Your kind note accompanying the present pierced me to the quick. You said you would visit me and shake me by the hand once again before we died. It spoke volumes. It shall be sincerely clasped. I know of no man, save Hudson Gurney, whose esteem I more truly value and always did, than yourself.' Then in the autumn he gathered up his sketching things and descended on Norfolk for a fortnight's holiday with Bulwer. The fortnight was prolonged to a month, two months. He drew churches with Bulwer, he made trips on the river, he renewed old acquaintances, he was fêted by his son's friends, he visited Dawson Turner at Yarmouth to whom he had written from Norwich: 'I have been sketching on our River, and at Hanworth, Cromer and Sheringham, the wilderness of Norfolk. . . . I came here really for my health. Judge for yourself my happiness on finding your Norfolk flints capable of once more creating a blaze in my heart.' And later of this trip he wrote: 'Oh! rare and beautiful Norfolk'.

None of the brilliant and moving series of drawings he made on this holiday was turned into water-colour. Many were in crayon, some in lead pencil, a few have a little heightening colour, two at least he began to develop in oil, but that was all. They are extraordinarily powerful and evocative fragments and show that Cotman had renewed yet again his vision in the presence of nature and was at the beginning of another phase of development. But in January the black cloud again descended and by July he was dead. There was no disorder of the body, only one of the spirit which could endure no more.

Cotman is an enigma. He saw himself as a landscapist of the School of Gaspard Poussin; as an etcher he claimed to follow Piranesi; and some of his rare figure-studies derive from Salvator Rosa. Yet, though the romantic vision of all three was present in his work, it is always (save in his charcoal or chalk sketches) tormented by an essentially classical discipline and restraint, a classical respect for means and method quite unlike the apparent character of the man. As a romantic he loved ruins and found it difficult to respond to buildings that were unimproved by the gentle smears of time, but though he selected his angle of vision as carefully as Piranesi in order to squeeze the utmost drama from it, he rarely seems to have concerned himself with the passion inherent in his subject, but to have concentrated his mind upon the elaborate simplicity of his constructions. His pictures are rarely without what at that period was called 'effect', but the 'effect' is not often of an importance comparable to the sense of proportion and arrangement in the picture. Often indeed the very features which are designed to produce the 'effect' are themselves caught up in the process of pattern-making and become part of it, so that even in the extreme instance of *Storm on Yarmouth Beach* (Plate 38a), where the storm-cloud looms above the struggling men and the darkness falls and the gale begins, we are quite as conscious of the strange shape of the drama as we are of the drama itself. And in *Greta Bridge* (Oppé, Plate VIII), where the calm of evening pervades its horizontality and we know that the space over the water is filled with the evening noises of birds catching flies, we still find much of our pleasure in the lines *as* lines, and the spaces *as* spaces.

It seems possible to isolate eleven distinct manners in Cotman's water-colours. This classification, which has only a rough validity, should help in the dating of his work and may serve to correct a tendency to take drawings from him which are properly his. (1) The Academic Period with predominant russet colouring, 1799–1800 (Plates 28a, 30a). (2) The Sketch Club drawings, 1800–4. These are given homogeneity throughout the period by the type of subject, the material used, and the conditions under which they were done (Kitson, Plates 7 and 8). (3) The Blue Period, 1800–2. Girtin's influence is at its height (Plates 28b, 29a, 29b). (4) The Period of Chinese Delicacy. This is the very personal stage which seems to arise from the Sketch Club work, and is closer to some work by Paul Sandby Munn than to that of any other contemporary artist (Plate 30b).[1] This style includes a number of very delicately-drawn landscapes with an unfinished, sometimes slightly meagre, appearance (Kitson, Plate 20). Its culmination is in the Rokeby drawings but it continues for a while into the first Norwich period, 1801–7 (Plates 29a, 29b). (5) The Deep-toned Period, 1807–12, when Cotman—in common with other water-colourists—painted 'up' to oils. (Plates 32b, 33a, 33b). (6) The Normandy Period, not rich in water-colour but marked chiefly in its later days by his sepia landscapes and his elaborate architectural drawings (Plate 35b). During this period the gold and blue manner develops. (7) The Gold and Blue manner, of which a premonition appeared in *Study of Trees, Harrow* (Plate 30b) as early as 1805, became well-developed about 1820, and was continued in various sub-forms until nearly the end of his life (Plate 36a). The 'Toledo' style *c.* 1828–36, best named after a well-known example of it (Oppé, Plate XVIII) is really a branch of the Gold and Blue manner in which those colours in their least accommodating form are applied to 'splendid' scenes of foreign cities. The drawings

[1] Although this picture is also the nearest Cotman ever came to Crome.

are nearly always 'after' the sketches of travellers such as W. H. Harriott (1811–46), a pupil of Prout, and Bulwer, but the style includes such imaginative horrors as *The Rose of Flixton*. It is in fact a marriage of gold and blue colour with drawing in the Normandy manner. (8) The Pseudo-classical Romantic manner (Plate 38b) 1833, is an offshoot of the Gold and Blue style in which an attempt is made to lose his firm sense of form in a Turneresque miasma. (9) Figure Drawings in the manner of Rosa. These are not common and appear from their manner to be *c.* 1810 but some were done much later for King's College. (10) The attempt at Conventional Vision which appears spasmodically from 1824–34 (Plates 36b, 37a). There are various manifestations of this, of which one type is often and easily confused with the work of his son Miles Edmund (*A Glade with a Heron*—Birmingham City Art Gallery—*Old Water Colour Society Club*, Vol. XVI, Plate XIII). (11) The 'paste-medium moorland landscapes, *c.* 1835 (Plate 40a) and Oppé Plates XIX–XXIV, in which tone and mood are generally sombre but which are usually lit by a patch of vivid colour. These are amongst his finest achievements.

The inadequacy of even this attempted classification is shown by the difficulty of fitting in such intensely felt creations as *The Via Mala* (Plate 39a), *The Needles* (Kitson, Plate 88), and *The Dismasted Brig* (Kitson, Plate 109).

Such a variety of modes of expression argues artistic vitality; but it is also true that the work of most other major water-colourists would yield comparable surprises to those who have learned to associate only one manner with one name. If Cotman changed direction more often and more violently than others it was because his nature demanded the intoxication of success, or the dream of it, and his search led him into strange places. His dilemma was somewhat the same as, in another field, was that of the architect Sir John Soane; he was at heart a classical artist who had the misfortune to work in the full fury of a romantic age.[1]

The death of Cotman, unlike his moves to and from Norwich, was not in itself a milestone in the development of the School. Had he lived he might have created new forms, but to Norwich his inheritance had already passed through the hands of his sons, Miles Edmund and John Joseph, and through his pupils. Nevertheless, the years 1839 to 1843 did form an epoch that marked the end of the old order.

In 1839 John Thirtle died. His work shows little change over the years although occasionally one comes across a drawing in which the colours are clearer, the washes more simple, and the subject chosen less for its obvious appeal than usual. But these are so

---

[1] Such labels require definition. There is too little agreement upon their meaning. For example Professor Pevsner appears to regard Soane as 'highly romantic'; but so have many people regarded Cotman.

much the exception and so little like the usual Thirtle that one is in half a mind whether to accept them as his or no and one finds oneself thinking of James Stark (Plate 19b). They are probably late work.

Sillett died in 1840, and Robert Ladbrooke in 1842, but they had long since ceased to have any noticeable effect upon the work of their fellow artists. Both were of the eighteenth century and the eighteenth century had now long been buried beneath the experimentalism and the brash self-confidence of the Industrial Revolution.

John Berney Crome having retreated bankrupt from Norwich settled in Yarmouth and died there in 1842. So slight is his personality as a water-colourist that any work of distinction which time may uncover will probably be attributed to others.

A greater loss than these was that of the amateur E. T. Daniell. Daniell had moved to London to the curacy of St Mark's, South Audley Street at the end of 1833 at about the same time that Cotman left the city. Here he lived the sociable life of a young patron, entertaining such men as Turner, Landseer, Eastlake, Mulready, and Roberts, and exhibiting his own work at the Royal Academy and at the British Institution. The sight of Roberts's drawings of Egypt and Palestine roused emulation in him; he resigned his curacy and in the autumn of 1840 was sketching in the Adriatic and the Aegean. For the next two years he moved about the Middle East until in September 1842 he died of fever in Asia Minor.

The drawings made on these tours are free pen sketches on buff paper washed-in broadly with a limited palette. Whether he intended to develop them as oil-paintings, as water-colours, or as etchings is not clear. They impress with their freedom and their economy of means, but sometimes breadth becomes emptiness and the coloured paper, as always, is unsympathetic to paint. The cumulative effect of 120 of these large sketches at Norwich Castle and a further sixty-four at the British Museum is at first dispiriting (Plates 65b, 66). Nevertheless, amongst them, though they were perhaps intended for no eyes but his own, are some powerful drawings. His starting-point, the drawings made by Cotman about 1820, is still recognizable but the hand and eye now have a peculiar quality which is only his. Daniell's reputation rests upon his etchings, but his water-colours should not be ignored.

Although these six men died within four years, and all those who founded the Norwich Society in 1803 were gone, the city continued to be an active art centre.

The senior of the survivors were now Henry Ninham and James Stark. Ninham had worked largely as an engraver and his water-colours are too meagre to enable one to chart his development. The main influence on his work seems to have been that of the Cotman interiors of about 1806—there is a not dissimilar use of delicate colour and fine drawing.

Occasionaly, as in *A Thatched Cottage* (Plate 42b)[1] in the British Museum, there is a trim echo of Dixon and of Thirtle, but although he lived until 1874 there is no sign that any later developments affected him. His range was small, his draughtsmanship moderate, his colour sensitive but weak, and altogether he is one of the least satisfying of the School (Plate 42a).

James Stark as an oil-painter was the most typical of the pupils of Crome but as a water-colourist he was rather more. The rather too 'appealing' nature of some of his oils gives way to a more sincere and clumsy vision as though in water-colour he set out not to please but to learn and record.

When his apprenticeship ended Stark left for London, where he studied in the Royal Academy Schools but continued to exhibit at Norwich as well as in Town. In 1821, the year Crome died, he had already been in London for seven years but now returned to Norwich and took part in the collective activities there. His chief work during the latter half of this his second Norwich period was in preparation for *Scenery of the Rivers of Norfolk* with thirty-six plates, which did not appear until four years after his second London period began in 1830. Although he never again lived in Norwich Stark kept in touch with his native place; and when yet another attempt was made to form a society of artists (The Norfolk and Norwich Art Union with Leman as secretary) he sent regularly to its exhibitions. In 1859 he died. His son, A. J. Stark (1831–1902), who specialized in animal studies, shows at times a surprising talent but has little to do with Norwich.

David Hodgson also survived until 1863 but his water-colours are very few. A modest and amiable man, he printed privately in 1860 *A Reverie or Thoughts Suggested by a Visit to the Gallery of Deceased Norfolk and Norwich Artists* in verse as honest and as bad as his painting in oils. This pamphlet and the loan exhibition which was its occasion show how strongly the artists of Norwich had convinced themselves that they were a community with a common aim and a corporate entity.

Leman and Lound continued for nearly twenty years after Cotman's death to be the pivot of the Norwich artists. Lound, who died in 1861, was not a positive influence in the new developments of the School but rather a constant reminder of its past. Leman, on the other hand, who died two years after Lound in 1863, was drawing with a stronger line and with clearer, brighter washes in a way that was related to Middleton and yet was his own (Plate 57, Colour Plate IV).

Colkett died in the same year as Leman. From 1828 to 1836 he had lived in London but then returned to Norwich as a dealer, restorer, and drawing-master, where he stayed for seven years before transferring his business to Yarmouth and eventually, for the last ten years of his life, to Cambridge. His was a slight talent but he deserves to be remem-

[1] If it is his.

Plate VIII *Alby, Norfolk* John Middleton (1827–1856)

bered for it rather than as a poor imitator and copyist of Stark and an over-painter of Cotman's canvasses, which is all Dickes could say of him.

Alfred Priest, who was of similar age to Geldart, Freeman, and the Cotman sons, had moved to London in the early thirties but returned to Norwich in 1848 and died two years later. Most of his known work is in oils, and his surviving water-colours are too few to tell whether they came to owe anything to his master, Stark. Probably there was little work of any sort done in his later years, as he is said to have taken to brandy.

Obadiah Short died as late as 1886, and John Berney Ladbrooke continued to live at Norwich until his death in 1879; but for many years neither had stood in the forefront of the movement.

The men who were the expression of what was fresh and vigorous in the art of Norwich, Joseph Geldart, Miles Edmund Cotman, W. P. B. Freeman, John Joseph Cotman, and Henry Bright, were born between 1810 and 1814 and had few roots in Crome.

Geldart figures often in the correspondence of the period and although his water-colours are unknown his influence, particularly on J. J. Cotman, was considerable. In a pathetic journal which John Joseph began to keep in 1838 he admits the importance of Geldart to him: 'At this time I met a new friend whom I admired and strove to imitate.' And again in 1838, when his repeatedly renewed resolutions to mend his ways and to lead a regular and industrious life as repeatedly broke down, he wrote: 'Good accounts from Joseph at Florence. I am almost afraid to say that I count on his return. I have since his time gone back *far far*.' The journal was not continued and their future relationship is unknown, but it would not be usual if such a friendship based on psychological dependence lasted for long. Their art showed a common violence of vision. Geldart's chalk drawings are vigorous and dramatic and his interest in colour—he is described as sitting in the piazza at Venice demonstrating Venetian colour principles on the café table-top—is reflected in the very individual colour of John Joseph.

Both the artist sons of John Sell Cotman had suffered in their several ways from their father's energetic and erratic domination. Miles Edmund, the loyal lieutenant, eventually became his father's recognized and paid assistant at King's College. An attempt to secure for him the post of Professor of Drawing at the City of London School failed in 1836. In 1841 a move towards marriage was promptly vetoed by his father on the grounds of economic impossibility. After his father's death he found that the succession to the professorship did not automatically fall upon him; but he did achieve it (as well as marriage), and remained in London teaching until 1852 when for some undisclosed reason he was unable to retain the post. His application for other appointments being unsuccessful he returned to Norfolk. He taught at North Walsham for some years before going to live with his brother in Norwich until his death in 1858. It is difficult to detect development in Miles Edmund's water-colours. He quickly mastered a decisive line, strong colour, and a certain trimness of finish, which served him well. His work seems to have sold more readily than his father's, but it achieved no particular success in his life time and has been underestimated since.

John Joseph Cotman, after the brief interlude as his father's assistant in London, spent the remainder of his life in Norwich. There were recurrent difficulties. His wish to marry, like his brother's, was firmly stamped on; but he persisted and some years after his father's death married the girl who had been denied him. As the century advanced fewer people took private drawing lessons and the greater part of a drawing-master's income came from institutional teaching. Yet his income from this source, which soon after his father left Norwich sank to £100 a year, he raised at one time to £300. John Joseph's unstable temperament, his depressions and constant self-criticism, led to periods of excessive drinking; but the Cotmans were none of them without courage and the fight to mend his life never ceased. In 1838 his father wrote to him, very significantly from one who had himself made the same mistake:[1] 'If you wish to be an artist you must leave Norwich, for nothing can be done for you there. Give up Norwich and all its little associations, and put yourself under me. I am now willing and able to lead you. I won't ask of you more than four hours a day—the rest shall be your own. Your duty and respect I ask of you as a parent. You shall have free use of opinion and differ from me as much as you please—but let that difference be given as a man. I feel that I have on this point been woefully misunderstood: I have never wished implicit agreement to my opinion, but I have been repeatedly angry at your mode of expressing opposition.' John Joseph wisely remained in Norwich and struggled on with the help of his friends there. Some pupils must have continued with him and he must have sold some pictures, for despite crises of debt and sale such as his father had known he maintained himself after a fashion until his death in 1878. He seems to have been like his father in his capacity to arouse affection in his friends and to have had even more than his father a capacity to exasperate them beyond endurance. A terrible letter from one of them is in the Reeve Collection. It is typical of John Joseph that he preserved this letter all his life. In 1858, the year of his brother's death, his wife and family left him; they too were unable to endure the recurrent periods of headlong drinking when every asset within sight was sold or pawned to satisfy his need. From these bouts he emerged to struggle on, drawing and teaching. In 1862 his sister Anne died,

[1] It is true that in over thirty years the position had substantially changed and the pull of London had become more apparent. Yet it was in 1840 that Cox moved from London to Harbourne; he, however, retained a substantial London market and in any case Birmingham by 1840 had left Norwich far behind.

leaving him £500 which lasted only a short while. Norwich knew him well as a character, eccentric in dress, gait, and behaviour. When he came to die in Norwich Hospital he was in complete destitution. One friend alone attended him, James Reeve the Museum Curator, and it was Reeve who paid for his coffin.

John Joseph continued to be a firm and fluent draughtsman with more freedom and passion than his brother Miles, but as the years passed he became increasingly committed to a highly personal range of colour in which gold, blue, and indian red predominate. To an eye attuned to the muted tones of the 'Greta' drawings, or to the work of any of the masters of the first ten years of the nineteenth century, the first sight of a J. J. Cotman in full colour may come as a shock or a revelation. The blues and golds are obviously based on his father's use of the same colours, but he sometimes used them with more subtlety and richness of effect and often more appropriately than his father had done. His landscapes of autumn or high summer are drenched in a strange richness of hue which is not the result of a formula but of a sensuous joy in the colours themselves—as though, like his father, he would have delighted to pour jewels through his hands so that they mingled with brocaded silks, pictures by Rubens and autumn leaves, in a pile at his feet (Colour Plate VII). There is something of Samuel Palmer's later drawings about them, as there is something of Palmer's greater days in John Joseph's great foliage pictures (Plates 74, 75a). His range was not wide, nor are his drawings all equally successful, but he is one of the most remarkable and least appreciated water-colourists of the third quarter of the century.

To turn from John Joseph Cotman to W. P. B. Freeman (1813–97) is to descend to a very different plane of achievement. Freeman was an amateur who derived his colour from John Sell Cotman's drawings of 1824 in a milk-and-water sort of way. His landscapes, in which he tried to use John Joseph's russet in combination with green, fail because he lacked breadth of vision and his draughtsmanship was not good; but in seascapes he was more successful, and the use of cobalt which is almost like a signature tune in Freeman's pictures is not unpleasing in spacious marine skies (Plate 70b).

The latest comer to the list of Norwich School men, and one who has recently come to be highly regarded, was John Middleton (1827–56). Middleton is generally considered in conjunction with Henry Bright, who was seventeen years his senior, but whereas Bright was a Suffolk man and of Norwich only by adoption, Middleton was born in Norwich and was bred deep in its tradition. His father was a painter-decorator, his mother an amateur who exhibited flower-pieces at the Norwich Society. His first masters were John Berney Ladbrooke and Joseph Stannard; he was close to and learned from Henry Bright; he admired and was the friend of Lound. Although it is not recorded that he learned from Stark there is at times a certain similarity in the clearness of their colour and the clear-cut incisive outline of their forms. It is as though the qualities of these, and indeed of all the Norwich men, fused between 1846 and 1849 to produce a brilliant but short efflorescence. Bright, Leman and Lound all gave startling expression to the new vision, but none more successfully than Middleton.

The drawings of Middleton's prime, if we may call it so—for like Watteau and Keats he was a young consumptive—have often the spirit of Crome in their passionate affection for green growth and sunlit glimpses between trees, but the manner is now that of a water-colourist in the great tradition. Bright may have taught him some tricks in the use of water-colour but Bright himself had not yet been infected with the passion for concealing the material in which the artist worked, and no harm was done. No other water-colourist in England in the middle of the century so clearly understood and delighted in the potentialities of his medium as did Middleton, and indeed no other artist save Cotman himself in his 'Greta' period ever used water-colour so purely; and even he never used the white of his paper with such boldness.

Middleton came into his heritage early. He was only 20 when the *Norfolk Chronicle*[1] linked his name with Etty, Frith, and Müller, and referred to him as 'one of the most rising young artists of the day', praising the 'brilliancy of colouring, charming alternation of light and shade, admirable drawing and grouping' of his pictures. His *Alby, Norfolk* (Colour Plate VIII) is dated 1847 and makes a fascinating comparison with Cotman's *Dropgate* (Kitson, Plate 31) of forty-two years earlier and his *Shadowed Stream* (Kitson, Plate 141) of about 1837. In Middleton's picture we are more directly involved in the emotion of the scene, the receding backwater, the sunlight and the shadow, the reflections on the still surface; we can hear the water-voles moving under the bank, and the insects humming about the hot foliage, and somewhere behind us in the meadow cattle are pulling noisily at lush grass. It is easy to forget that we are looking at a picture, because it has caught us up so completely in its world of summer sunshine. With neither of Cotman's drawings is it quite the same. The thoughts, sensations, memories, are certainly there but they are less apparent; our greatest pleasure is not in them but in the fact that the forms are thus and thus, linking, echoing, like music, with strange assurance and harmony forming a pattern that the eye delights to linger upon. Robert Leman's *The Water Gate* (Plate 57) has something of the quality of both. Middleton's *Tonbridge* (Plate 77b) dates from the same high summer for it is very close to Henry Bright's *Old Barn* (Colour Plate VI) and to Bright's dated *Barn* in Norwich Castle; it is likely that the two men went sketching together in Kent in this year. Neither of them reached greater heights than

[1] 11 December 1847.

this. The directness with which Middleton captured these arcadian days gives to these pictures something of the lyrical quality of Cotman's 'Greta Woods' drawings. Middleton's idyll was as quickly over. In the years after 1849 little of his quality remains; the brilliant colour, the confident drawing became hard and formal, his vision becomes a trick, the poetry has gone and he rarely again succeeded in penetrating so surely to the heart of his subject as during the summers of 1846, 1847, and 1848.

Middleton often inscribed his drawings with date and place. I have seen no earlier date than 1846 which is on *Richmond* at Norwich Castle and on my own *Near Butterdale* (Plate 78b). These are in his fully-developed style, other undated drawings such as two in the possession of Mr E. P. Hansell give the impression of being earlier. They can hardly have been much earlier, for in 1846 he was no more than 19. In 1847 there are a succession of great water-colours of Kent, where he visited Tonbridge, Tunbridge Wells, and Lullingstone.[1] In 1848 there is no record of a distant sketching trip although it is likely that one was made; the only dated drawing is of *Hatfield*. In 1850 he was in Lynmouth in Devon. In 1852 he made a study in water-colour of Weybourne on the Norfolk coast. At some time he visited Arran. There is no drawing dated later than 1852.

Middleton moved to London in 1847 but returned to Norwich in 1849 and continued to base himself upon the city until his death in 1856.[2] It is not known whether he taught, and his influence is directly apparent in his own day only in the work of Lound and perhaps of Leman, whose quick apprehension made a better 'Middleton' of Snowdon (Colour Plate IV) than Middleton himself ever achieved with mountain forms. Here and there outside the Norwich circle as in the work of Henry Jutsum (1816–48), a pupil of Stark and friend of Bright, one finds unmistakable indications of an influence which is certainly similar to that of Middleton and which suggests that its true source was perhaps in Stark. There are also sketches by William Callow (1812–1900) that are almost pure Middleton in manner though without his inspiration. T. L. Rowbotham (1823–75) used a similar convention. Much later it is not fanciful to see an echo of this last great Norwich water-colourist in the broad washes of Wilson Steer.

There is not sufficient indication of what Middleton would have done had he lived. He painted a good deal in oil and would perhaps have done so increasingly. The later water-colours are more fussy and less pure and fresh in their washes. Probably the sixties would have been too much for him and his rare talent would have been sunk under the

---

[1] He appears to have spelled Tonbridge with a 'u' and Tunbridge Wells with an 'o'; a reversal of the accepted forms.

[2] Another J. Middleton who continued to exhibit in Norwich after his death may be his father or uncle; what his work was like is not recorded but it may, if signed, be a danger to collectors.

weight of fashionable 'finish'. He had seized upon one aspect of Bright's art and made it his own; so much so that one is momentarily astonished to find Bright's signature on the 'Barn' pictures. Perhaps, after all, the older man learned something from the younger, and Middleton owed less to Bright than we are inclined to think. The question of precedency will only be answered when water-colours by Bright, Leman, Lound and Middleton authentically dated 1845 can be seen together.

It would be satisfying to have shown how a coherent idea had run through the Norwich School, developing along natural lines of growth and passing on its traditions to vitalize the arts of today. Unfortunately, if there is one thing which has come clear from this brief inquiry, it is that there was originally not one Norwich tradition but two.

After The Norfolk and Suffolk Institution for the Promotion of Fine Arts disbanded Cotman wrote to Dawson Turner: 'On Saturday the full body of our decomposed Society of Artists met at my house for the last time. I deeply regret to find that Mr C. (John Berney Crome) fairly hinted it was a lost game to him. I deeply, deeply feel for him. . . .

'My oft-told *dream* terminated with the success of myself and my family and the downfall (in plain English) of the family of Crome. There is at this moment a fearful appearance of its being verified to the letter, for my prospects are to all appearances blooming and fresh, and—I deeply regret to say—the prospects of the Cromes are blighted and unsuccessful. Frederick died wretchedly; Miss Crome is about to leave Norwich in debt; William has already left Norwich, for no one to know where, in wretchedness and, I am afraid, insane—and so considered by his family.'

Cotman and Crome had no serious impact upon each other's work. Crome was the least personal, the least mannered of artists; Cotman the most individual and most original. As teachers perhaps Crome was more successful because he was less dogmatic and less intellectual. If his letter to Stark is typical it was his way to edge his pupils towards making their own discoveries; whereas Cotman taught his pupils to draw as he did. Crome took his pupils into the country; Cotman gave them his circulating portfolio. Each method has its appropriate results. Only strong personalities could emerge as individuals after Cotman's teaching and only strong personalities did, and even they bore scars. Crome's way, however, could cause a modest talent to yield its particular merit.

The men who followed the two famous masters were consequently no mere echoes of them. Echoes there no doubt were but they have been totally lost among those three hundred-odd exhibitors whose highest flights were 'after Crome' and 'after Cotman'. Those who came clear from the crowd, and there are perhaps others still to come, form a body of considerable artists who each explored his own 'avenue to excellence' and 'distinguished himself by some perfection which was to be found in himself only'.

Nor were Crome and Cotman the only influences; others taught in Norwich and other traditions were constantly at work there. Nor, despite its corporate spirit, had the School ever pretended to be self-contained: as it accepted influences from without so its own influences spread beyond East Anglia. Cox in one of his many varied moods was derivative from Cotman, whom he much admired (Plate 41a). The Varley brothers are rarely far from Cotman. The relationship of de Wint and Thirtle is deep-rooted, and conscious influence is almost certain. James Duffield Harding, the most popular drawing-master of the second quarter of the century, shows Cotman's influence and through him (ironically, for the 'Graduate of Oxford' never mentions his name) we can see something of Cotman's line in Ruskin, in Lewis, and in Lear. W. J. Müller, perhaps the most gifted water-colourist of the forties, acknowledged his debt to Cotman; while echoes of Henry Bright are widespread and frequent in the middle of the century.

But wherever we may detect the influence of Norwich in the work of other artists we must not allow ourselves to be deceived about the essential nature of the School. If we seek, as some have done, to see Norwich as the sole source of naturalistic landscape painting, we are falsifying the position. For a brief period of time the English artist and poet found himself face to face with natural scenery and saw it with the freshness of a child. It was a moment only, but a moment experienced by Wordsworth as well as by Crome, by Girtin as well as by Cotman, by Constable more perhaps than by any, and by a host of lesser men as well. Soon for most men the freshness departed; the vision tired and needed revivifying with subjective qualities, or it developed mannered formulae, or lost itself under layers of sentiment. The Norwich men kept closer to the simple revelation than many.

What then was the Norwich School if it was not the initiator and standard-bearer of a special type of landscape painting? The answer is that it was a community of artists who shared the common spirit of the time but who, inheriting a local tradition of fine craftsmanship in the visual arts, by learning from each other, and by drawing their inspiration from the same country-side, developed a corporate sense. The best of its pictures are strongly marked by a self-effacing attempt to distil from that countryside pictures 'which charm we know not why'.

Appendices

About any major group of painters there gathers a host of imitators, pupils, and minor personalities who are usually ignored. Very often the work of these lesser men is attributed by collectors to the masters themselves with the doubly unfortunate result that the master's artistic personality is confused and the small man who produced meritorious work sinks into oblivion.

In preparation for the Norwich Exhibition of the Fine Arts for 1860 the Committee issued a letter asking for the loan of pictures by deceased Norwich artists. Many of those we have discussed in this book were still living and did not qualify, but there were forty-four names on their list which were presumably all who at that time were considered worthy of remembrance. Some of these forty-four have been omitted from this book because they worked only in oils, others because they were miniature-painters or portraitists like Horacé Beevor Love (1800–38).[1] But what has happened to the work of the twenty-three artists in the list whose names have not even been mentioned? Nor should we forget that, by 1828, 323 individuals had contributed to the Norwich exhibitions of whom only forty-four were remembered for the Memorial Exhibition. Even if we allow that a further forty were not eligible because they were still alive it means that only a quarter of the exhibitors had survived as artistic personalities in their native city thirty-two years later.

It would be unprofitable to attempt to raise all these dead, but some of them who may have worked in water-colour and some also who never

exhibited at Norwich but were close in spirit should not be lost sight of by the inquiring collector.

HENRY BAINES (1823–94), who was born at King's Lynn was intended as a sailor, but going to London studied under Etty and Landseer. He returned to Lynn about 1850 where he took pupils—including some of the Gurney family. His work varies but is always individual, with a character at times reminiscent of Etty and at times of J. J. Cotman (Plate 77a).

In the exhibition of 1805 there was a J. BLAKE who was probably related to an R. Blake whose sketchbook of rather precise over-detailed drawings has recently been dispersed. They were connected with the Gurney family as were the Bells, Birkbecks, and Geldarts, all names which recur as amateurs or collectors and help to show how strong the Quaker influence (though they were not all Friends) was likely to be upon the Norwich School.

E. BELL was a founder-member of the Society but may have been only an engraver. He moved to Worcester but remained an Honorary Member for many years. He was a pupil of Charles Hogdson.

'MR BERKELEY' was a drawing-master in Norwich in 1839 who claimed to have sixty pupils.

J. BORROW: see Appendix F.

F. B. BURRELL was a topographer. Nothing is recorded of him but he may be related to Joseph Francis Burrell, who exhibited in London between 1801 and 1854. There are some landscape sketches by J. F. Burrell in the Victoria and Albert.

JOSEPH CLOVER (1779–1853) was a portrait painter who earns a passing mention here because of a considerable number of water-colour

[1] Yet even these may have to be restored to the list if, as is far from unlikely, they are found to have produced a measurable quantity of water-colour landscapes.

landscapes in his sketchbooks at Norwich Castle. These vary a good deal. He is generally a good draughtsman but unambitious; the best group of his water-colours is dated 1810 and 1811; they are in a sort of Dixon × Thirtle manner which is not unpleasing.

EDWIN W. COOPER (fl. 1803–*ob.* 1833) worked chiefly at Newmarket where he painted oil-portraits of horses and dogs. Two water-colours signed and dated 1803 of horses in a landscape are the key to his work. They are delightfully fresh and lead to the identification of a landscape water-colour, which from its technique seems to be earlier, and which suggests that Cooper may have drawn portraits of houses as well as of horses (Plates 21a, 21b). Apart from these and a number of oils, I have seen only some pencil sketches and fragments of water-colour in Norwich Castle, and a fairly large *Landscape with Sporting Dogs and Game*, signed and dated 1824, in Messrs Appleby's Exhibition for December 1964. There is probably a good deal of his work in horse-loving houses.

DANIEL COPPIN, another founder-member, contributed pictures 'after Barker of Bath' to the first exhibition. In 1814 he went with Crome on his jaunt to Paris. He was President of the Norwich Society in 1816. Dickes speaks well of him as a landscape painter. His wife also painted and it was his daughter who married Joseph Stannard. I have found no water-colours but they probably exist.

Another Norwich name recurs in Victoria Colkett who became Mrs Hine. She was perhaps the daughter of Samuel David Colkett. There are two pictures by her in Norwich Castle; one signed *V.C.* 1862 is of St Peter Mancroft and is a little reminiscent of W. P. B. Freeman (Cot. and Haw., page 94, Plate 16); the other is a rather weak 'Ninhamish' affair. She was still living in 1860 when she exhibited several architectural views of Cambridge.

Three lesser known members of the Crome family were also artists; Frederick James (1796–——) became a bank clerk but was an amateur etcher; Emily (1801——) exhibited still-life and flower-pieces at Norwich, and in London, her work was probably in oils; and William Henry (1806——) who exhibited oils. Did they do no water-colours?

J. DONTHORNE of the 1860 list is presumably the Johnny Donthorne who was Con-stable's assistant and who also worked as a picture cleaner. He died of consumption in 1832. His work was probably in oils.

MRS FREWER was a founder-member who contributed *A Magdalen after Guido* and *An Auricula from Nature* to the first exhibition.

J. GOOCH is the painter of a rather colourless and too delicately-drawn water-colour in my own collection (Plate 22a) which has led to the identification of the painter of *Carrow Bridge* (Plate 22b). A 'Mr Gooch' exhibited in 1812; a 'Mr B. Gooch' exhibited in 1813; a 'J. Gooch' had a large number of exhibits in 1814 and 1815 and again in the following year, when a Mr C. Gooch also appears. The *Norfolk Chronicle* of 29 July 1820 recommends 'Mr G. Gooch' . . . 'to improve himself as a colourist.' In 1824 the same paper said of his composition . . . 'there is not much that is striking about it' although they had praise for his 'appropriate warmth of colour and neatness of finish'. A James or John Gooch exhibited at the British Institution between 1819 and 1833 from an address at Norwich until 1825 and at Twickenham thereafter. An Archdeacon John Gooch lived in Suffolk and is known by some feeble etchings. J. Gooch was represented only by an oil *Landscape with Sheep* in the Memorial Exhibition of 1860. It is not improbable that the varying initials apply to one man, or at the most to two.

THE REVEREND W. GORDON was an exhibitor at the first meeting and a Ladbrooke secessionist. He is said to have been a landscape-painter.

C. H. HARRISON (1842–1902) of Yarmouth worked in the typical late Victorian manner. There is a detailed water-colour dated 1882 by him in Norwich Castle for which little good can be said. An exhibition of his work was held at Great Yarmouth in 1903.

HARRY HINE was perhaps connected with the Hine who married Victoria Colkett. His work is above average. In Norwich Castle there is a sensitive landscape by him dated 1876; its clean drawing, delicate colouring, and unaffected rendering of a pleasant scene would do credit to many better-known painters (Plate 80b). A very detailed gouache in a much higher key which I have seen attributed to him is, however, a different matter.

Two water-colour sketches of houses at Acle

near Great Yarmouth signed and dated 1875 reveal the existence of a C. HINE. They are freely drawn and washed with tarry-yellows and browns, not altogether pleasing. They seem to be related to the work of 'W. Rowland' and of Rose Winter.

HENRY JUTSUM (1816–69) was born in London, became an Associate of the New Water Colour Society in 1843, but resigned five years later. In 1839 he became a pupil of James Stark. He seems latterly to have devoted himself to oils and his water-colours are not common. Those I have seen are instantly relatable to Bright and Middleton but with a more conventional late nineteenth-century finish. If one can accept the convention, and there is no real reason why one should not, he seems to have been an able if unadventurous painter who would repay attention (Plate 76b).

In Norwich Castle there is a water-colour 'after Ninham' by J. PATIENCE, which certainly has some of the quality of Ninham. The only other Patience I have seen is 'after J. S. Cotman'; it has tell-tale bad passages. He is otherwise unknown, but if as a copyist he were (as he may well have been) just a little better than in these two drawings, it is not surprising that work under his name is not to be seen.

HUMPHREY REPTON, 1752–1818, was a successful landscape-gardener who owed at least some of his popularity to the *Red Books* which he produced for his clients. These, by means of ingeniously overlapping water-colour sketches, showed them their grounds before and after treatment. He is a competent if slight water-colourist.

'W. ROWLAND' is the signature of Rowland Winter, an oddly neglected artist. He is known as 'of Yarmouth' and the water-colours of his I have seen are of Yarmouth buildings. He is said to have been born in 1851 and would if so have done his most mature work at the age of 9, for his *North Quay and Townhall Great Yarmouth* (Plate 80a) has an 'Old Master' look and is dated 1860. Judging from his style, which has something of the breadth—though not the tonal strength—of Robert Dixon, Rowland may have been a theatrical scene-painter. There are some strange topographical prints of Yarmouth dated 1915 by 'Rose Winter' which are surely by 'W. Rowland' or a faithful pupil. The hand is now that of an old man. There are several possible explanations, the obvious one being that he was born in, say, 1831 and that if a W. Rowland was born in 1851 it was his son. This would make the 1915 sketches the work of a man of 84, which they well might be. What is quite impossible is that the 1860 pictures were done by a nine-year-old.

It is not certain what relationship there is between 'W. Rowland' and the C. J. W. WINTER (1820–91) whose neat, painstaking, antiquarian work is in the Bulwer Collection at Norwich Castle. (Cot. and Haw. 111., page 86, Plate 21.)

MICHAEL SHARP, the friend of Crome, is really a Londoner, though his name crops up frequently in the Norwich correspondence of the time. He was a figure-painter and a portraitist who may have worked only in oil.

JOHN WILLIAM SHELLEY (1838–70) and ARTHUR SHELLEY (1841–1902) were both of Yarmouth. In the back of a large sketch book of J. W. Shelley presented to Norwich Castle in 1936 by the artist's granddaughter, Lady Mundy, is a list of places and dates which may represent sketching tours. He was at Yoxford in 1861, London (the Exhibition) in 1862, Isle of Man 1863, Plymouth and Cornwall 1864, Ullswater in 1865, Yoxford and Plymouth 1866, Chislehurst and Holne 1867, Windsor 1868, Mortlock 1869, and Plymouth in 1870. His water-colours are fresh and dainty in colour, quite pretty but with the flavour of a clever amateur. Arthur Shelley was perhaps his brother. There is one water-colour of his at Norwich Castle: a fine detailed landscape in the late Victorian sentimental vein. There is no evidence that these men were related to the distinguished water-colourist Samuel Shelley (1750–1808) who was a Londoner.

FRANCIS STEVENS 'of Exeter' was a capable water-colourist, distinguished enough to be elected an Associate of the Water-Colour Society in 1805 and a Member four years later, and yet one whose work is now rarely seen—at least under its right name. His master was Paul Sandby Munn, through whom no doubt arose an acquaintance with Cotman. He does not seem to have been a Norwich man and his earliest exhibited pictures were of Devon and of the neighbourhood of Wortley in Yorkshire (Plate 26b). In 1810 he became a Member of the Norwich Society, probably through Cotman's influence. In 1816 he appears to have been teaching at the Military College, Sandhurst, and later his address was at Exeter. In 1808 he had etched a series of *Views of Cottages and Farmhouses in England and Wales* after drawings by Munn, Varley, Hills, Pugin, Prout, and others. He was one of the original members of Chalon's Sketching Society of which the first meeting was held in his house in 1808. This long-lived body was heir to the Sketch Club of Girtin and Cotman. Stevens exhibited for the last time with the 'Old' Water Colour Society in 1823, at which date he was still an Honorary Member of the Norwich Society. Nothing more is known of him. He is a pastoral landscapist in the manner of Munn and to be distinguished from Munn of 1805–15 chiefly by harder handling. I have a water-colour of Raby Castle which echoes Cotman as well as Munn but which remains strongly individual. He seems to delight in the exquisite rendering of the brickwork of old chimney-stacks (Plate 27a).

There are several small topographical water-colours, clear, sharp, and bright, by G. S. STEVENSON in Norwich Castle. He was probably an amateur. John Ninham's *Gates of Norwich* were produced for William Stevenson, F.S.A., and were bought by the Norwich bookseller, Muskett, for J. W. Stevenson; presumably G. S. was of this family (Plate 59a).

W. TAYLOR of King's Lynn (1800–61) was born in London though his father was from Norfolk. He was for some years a schoolmaster, but in 1844 when the Lynn Museum was founded he became its secretary and remained so until his death. In 1848 he is recorded as running, in association with his son William Henry, a business as engraver, printer, publisher, and stationer. He published a number of books on local antiquities illustrated by himself. His water-colour *Purfleet* though more than a mere antiquary's drawing is rather hard (Plate 59b.

The last name which Dickes admits to the School is that of JAMES WILLIAM WALKER (1831–98). Walker was born at Norwich, was apprenticed to a painter-decorator, and was a pupil at the Norwich School of Design. He taught under the Department of Science and Art in London and later became Master of the School of Art at Bolton; he also at one time taught privately at Southport. Sketching tours are recorded in Lancashire, Cumberland, Wales and Brittany. In 1881 he went to Naples and to Rome. A large number of his drawings are in Norwich Castle, six in the British Museum, one in the Victoria and Albert but none in the Bolton Museum and Art Gallery. They are conventional water-colours typical of the latter half of the nineteenth century in their competent but banal approach to the prettiness of landscape. Although he was a Norwich man there is nothing in his work to show that he ever saw the work of John Crome or of the Cotmans.

C. J. WATSON (fl. *c.* 1880) seems on the strength of one or two water-colours I have seen to be professional in his competence but rather pedestrian. He appears to have been a follower of Thirtle.

WILLIAM WILKINS, R.A. (1778–1839). There are two Wilkins, the famous architect who perpetrated the National Gallery and numbers of buildings in Cambridge, and his father who was a plasterer and stucco worker in Norwich. Both did architectural and topographical drawings in the old stained drawing style (Cot. and Haw., page 62, Plate 5).

WILLIAM YETTS of Yarmouth painted some pictures which were lithographed by S. D. Colkett. He also did some engraving on his own account and may have done water-colours.

Zobell is the name of a family best known for their sand-pictures. J. G. ZOBELL, 1791–1879, exhibited at Norwich in 1819 and appears to have been chiefly a glass-painter. There are two large water-colours by him at the Castle and I have another of Sandling Ferry taken from a viewpoint similar to the sepia by Robert Ladbrooke (Plate 52b). The technique is quite distinct and not ineffective but it may not be fanciful to detect a relationship to the gritty restless surface which is typical of sand-pictures. There is some stained glass by him in Norwich Cathedral.

Besides these lesser-known East Anglian artists, a number of national figures not especially connected with Norwich occasionally exhibited with the Society. R. R. Reinagle, A.R.A., was an Honorary Member in 1816 and both he and his father exhibited in 1820. By 1830 the list of Honorary Members included the P.R.A., Sir Martin Shee, Sir William Beechey, R.A., Benjamin Haydon, R.A., Thomas

Churchyard, George Cattermole, and John Varley. In 1829 George Fennell Robson showed four pictures, and others who exhibited in that year were Augustus Wall Callcott, R.A., W. Clarkson Stanfield, R.A., W. H. Bartlett, and George Cattermole. Later William Etty, R.A., John Linnell, Henry Gastineau, and G. Clinch, A.R.A., showed pictures there. Of all these Sir William Beechey has most claim to be considered a Norwich man. His water-colour landscapes, of which there are a number in the British Museum, show neither sensibility nor skill and it is difficult to believe that Crome learned much from him (*see* Appendix E).

George Cattermole also has a faint claim to be considered of Norwich. He came from Diss in Norfolk and in 1816 an 'R' Cattermole exhibited five pictures. The initial may be a misprint or this 'R' may have been a relation. Later when five pictures by George were exhibited all but one came from the collection of

J. S. Cotman. This is revealing as it suggests that Cotman wished to raise the repute of the exhibition by the presence of such a famous name, and also that he was not averse from appearing in the guise of a patron and collector. Cotman's own excursions into mediaeval subjects are now shown to have their root in Cattermole rather than, as has been suggested, in Bonington. Cattermole's rare landscapes, for which today he is more generally esteemed by those who know them than for his later and more elaborate figure subjects, are sometimes in body-colour but when in pure water-colour they strongly reflect the manner of David Cox rather than of Cotman.

David Cox and his son were both represented in one of the Society's exhibitions but only 'from the Collection of J. S. Cotman'. Cox did, however, show seven drawings at Bury St Edmunds in 1828 when many Norwich men also exhibited.

APPENDIX B

James Reeve was the tenth curator of the Norwich Museum. He died in 1920 but his collection of notes, documents, and drawings of the Norwich School were acquired by the British Museum in 1902. Drawings which he collected in the last eighteen years of his life were frequently bought by R. J. Colman and subsequently passed with the Colman Collection to Norwich Castle. Reeve was born and bred in Norwich and knew some of the principal figures personally. He was notoriously outspoken in his comments upon false attributions, and as his standards were high and his means of gaining

information unequalled it has become almost axiomatic among students of the Norwich School that a Reeve attribution is unchallengeable. I suspect that he would not himself have subscribed to this view, for Reeve with all his opportunities was unlikely to have been right always: he did perhaps on occasions give more weight to tradition and to provenance than they can bear. There are examples about which even those who are less intrepid than the present author might well be doubtful; but in the main 'from the Collection of James Reeve' is a safe foundation on which to build.

APPENDIX C
(*Camera Lucida*)

It might be thought that the use of a *Camera Lucida* encouraged the development of Cotman's peculiar linear-outline type of patterning but he seems not to have used this instrument until his first Normandy tour in 1817, long after his characteristic style had been established. In a letter to Dawson Turner dated 12 June 1817 he says that Sir Harry Englefield had given him 'a Camera Lucida like yours,— they are used by all y artists I find! Chantrey

does everything by it, even to the splitting of a Hair.' (*Walpole Society*, Vol. XIV.)

The *Camera Lucida* is a fairly simple optical device whereby the virtual image of an object appears projected on paper where its outline can be traced. The credit for inventing this instrument is sometimes given to Cornelius Varley but it was, in fact, perfected by Dr W. H. Wollaston in 1807, and Varley only patented a specialized form of it known as 'Varley's Graphic

Telescope' in 1811. Cotman used one throughout his Normandy tour and yet another instrument was obtained for the use of the Turner girls when they joined him there. Once mastered it enabled complicated architectural drawings to be made quickly and accurately. Many of Cotman's Normandy pencil outlines done in this way are now in the possession of Dr J. S. Cotman; they form the basis of the well-known sepias of Normandy. The likeness of some of Cornelius Varley's drawings to Cotman is probably due to Varley's use of this instrument as well as to a similarity of artistic theory.

The *Camera Obscura* was known long before, having been developed in Italy in the sixteenth century. This throws a real image rather than a virtual one and, though used for drawing and copying, presented practical difficulties from which the *Camera Lucida* was free. Horace Walpole wrote in 1777: 'I have got a delightful plaything. . . . It is a new sort of camera-obscura for drawing the portraits of persons or prospects, or insides of rooms, and does not depend on the sun or anything. The misfortune is, that there is a vast deal of machinery and putting together . . . it has cost me ten guineas' . . . and later . . . 'It is such a perfecting of the camera obscura, that it no longer depends on the sun, and serves for taking portraits with a force and exactness incredible: and serves almost as well by candlelight as by day. It is called *the delineator*, and is invented within these eighteen months by a Mr Storer, a Norfolk man, one of the modestest and humblest of beings. Sir Joshua Reynolds and West are gone mad with it, and it will be their own faults if they do not excel Rubens in light and shade, and all the Flemish masters in truth. It improves the beauty of trees,—I don't know what it does not do.' (*Letters of Horace Walpole*, 7 July 1777 and 21 September 1777.) His enthusiasm was damped when the novelty wore off.

APPENDIX D

There are advantages in being educated to a reasonable standard of literacy. Crome who never leaves one in doubt of his intentions when drawing or painting is ambiguous in his one important surviving letter simply because he could not spell. His famous letter to his pupil and ex-apprentice, James Stark, written in January 1816, is fascinating not only because it tells us something of the principles on which Crome worked but because it reveals to us by our varied interpretations what *we* believe those essential principles to be:

'Friend James,

I received your kind letter and feel much pleased at your approval of my picture. I fear you will see too many errors for a painter of my long practice and at my time of life: however, there are parts in it you like, I have no doubt, so I am happy. You are likely to visit us (but mum is the order of the day about that concern), I wish it might be so; we shall be happy to see you in Norwich.

'In your letter you wish me to give you my opinion of your picture. I should have liked it better if you had made it more of a whole, that is, the trees stronger, the sky running from them in shadow up to the opposite corner; that might have produced what I think it wanted, and have made it a much less too picture effect. I think I hear you say, this fellow is very vain, and that nothing is right that does not suit his eye. But be assured what I have said I thought on the first sight, it strengthened me in that opinion every time I looked at it. (Honesty my boy!). So much for what it wanted; but how pleased I was to see so much improvement in the figures, so unlike our Norwich School; I may say they were good. Your boat was too small for them (you see I am at it again), but then the water pleased me, and I think it would not want much alteration in the sky. I cannot let your sky go off without some observation. I think the character of your clouds too affected, that is, too much of some of our modern painters, who mistake some of our great masters because they sometimes put in some of these round characters of clouds, they must do the same; but if you look at any of their skies, they either assist in the composition or make some figure in the picture, nay, sometimes play the first fiddle. I have seen this in Wouverman's and many others I could mention.

'Breath must be attended to, if you paint but

a muscle give it breath. Your doing the same by the sky, making parts broad and of a good shape, that they may come in with your composition, forming one grand plan of light and shade, this must always please the eye and keep the attention of the spectator and give delight to every one. Trifles in Nature must be overlooked that we may have our feelings raised by seeing the whole picture at a glance, not knowing how or why we are so charmed. I have written you a long rigmarole story about giving dignity to whatever you paint—I fear so long that I should be scarcely able to understand what I mean myself; you will, I hope, take the word for the deed, and at the same time forgive all faults in diction, grammar, spelling, etc. etc. etc.

'We have heard from John; I believe he is not petrified from having seen the French School. He says in his letter something about Tea-Tray painters. I believe most of those who visit them whistle the same note. So much for the French Artists.

'I hope they will arrive safe. Our happiness would be made complete "if your tongue could be heard amongst us". "Parley vous", my boy, will be echoed from garret to cellar in my house. I think I hear Vincent say to John: "Why, John, what d..d French rascal was that passed us just now? Why, look at his whiskers; why, he must be a Don Cossack." They had a charming voyage over Vincent belching as a steam packet much to the discomfiture of some of the other passengers. John did not say how Steel was in the passage, but I believe they were all bad alike.

'Sunday night—I put this last in my smooth paper epistle—that the boys are by my fireside going to take a glass of wine, quite well and happy. I wish you were with us. I have nothing more to say, only wishing you health and comfort.

Believe me, dear James,
Yours etc. etc.
JOHN CROME.'

It is all there. The man's transparent honesty of purpose, his kindliness, his quickness of apprehension, his feeling for air, for light, for balance, for breadth, his awareness of the Norwich group of painters as a corporate 'school', his contempt for prettiness and mannerism, none of this is in doubt *but* . . . did he mean by 'too picture' too picturesque an effect as Collins Baker, Keeper of the National Gallery, believed? Or did he mean a *two* picture effect as Sir Charles Holmes, Director of the National Gallery believed? The context suggests that Holmes was right but Collins Baker's interpretation is in a way even more true of Crome's way of thinking. And then again is 'breath' really 'breath' or is it 'breadth'? Surely the latter, but he *might* have meant by 'breath' life and air. Nor does Collins Baker help by suggesting that 'muscle' is a misspelling for 'mussel'!

APPENDIX E

There has been confusion about the frequency of Crome's visits to London. The question has some importance because if he visited London as frequently as he is alleged to have done we might expect to find more signs of metropolitan influence in his work than we do. The misunderstanding is based upon a well-known letter written by Sir William Beechey, R.A., after Crome's death: 'Crome, when first I knew him, must have been about twenty years old, and was a very awkward, uninformed country lad, but extremely shrewd in all his remarks upon Art, though he wanted words and terms to express his meaning. As often as he came to town he never failed to call upon me and to get what information I was able to give him upon the subject of that particular branch of Art which he had made his study. His visits were very frequent, and all his time was spent in my painting room when I was not particularly engaged. He improved so rapidly that he delighted and astonished me. He always dined and spent his evenings with me.'

Beechey, though born in Oxfordshire, is said to have worked for a house- and sign-painter in Norwich. This must have been before 1772 because in that year he was entered as a student in the Royal Academy. He certainly returned to Norwich in 1781 where he married his second wife and remained in practice as a portrait painter until 1786 when he went up to London to become a fashionable court-painter and R.A.

After the remove to London he kept alive his practice in Norwich and came back several times to paint portraits there. It is usually assumed that Beechey's evidence means that Crome made very frequent journeys to London. The fact that 'very frequent' journeys to London would have been difficult for a man in Crome's position has been strained at but swallowed. But surely by 'town' Beechey did not necessarily mean London? Beechey, meeting an uneducated youth at Harvey's home at Catton would not have known where he lived and might well assume he was a countryman from some Norfolk village. And 'about twenty years old' (this would make it 1788) is no more to be relied upon than 'lad' which would normally suggest a person younger than twenty. It is far more likely that Crome's visits to Beechey took place in Norwich and that they commenced towards the end of the period when Beechey still lived there—1781–86—and were continued on the occasions of Beechey's periodic return to the city.

APPENDIX F

The appearance of the name J. T. Borrow in the list of those whose works the Committee of 1860 wished to show in the Memorial Exhibition is interesting, for it is one of the few records of the brother of George Borrow who is addressed in the famous passage from *Lavengro*: 'A living master? Why, there he comes! Thou hast had him long; he has long guided thy young hand towards the excellence which is yet far from thee, but which thou canst attain if thou shouldst persist and wrestle, even as he has done midst gloom and despondency—ay, and even contempt; he who now comes up the creaking stair to thy little studio in the second floor to inspect thy last effort before thou departest, the little stout man whose face is very dark, and whose eye is vivacious; that man has attained excellence, destined some day to be acknowledged, though not till he is cold, and his mortal part returned to its kindred clay. He has painted, not pictures of the world, but English pictures, such as Gainsborough himself might have done; beautiful rural pieces, with trees which might well tempt the little birds to perch upon them. Thou needest not run to Rome, brother, where lives the old Mariolater, after pictures of the world, whilst at home there are pictures of England; nor needest thou even go to London, the big city, in search of a master, for thou hast one at home in the old East Anglian town who can instruct thee whilst thou needest instruction. Better stay at home, brother, at least for a season, and toil and strive midst groanings and despondency till thou hast attained excellence even as he has done—the little dark man with the brown coat and the top-boots, whose name will one day be considered the chief ornament of the old town, and whose works will at no distant period rank amongst the proudest pictures of England—and England against the world!—thy master, my brother, thy, at present, all-too-little considered master—Crome.'

John Borrow went to Rome and died there. Presumably he did not attain excellence, but if even a spark of his brother's extraordinary genius appeared in his pictures one would wish to see them. In 1819 he showed copies of Van Dyck and the Caracci at the Society's Exhibition. In 1824 he showed two portraits of which the critic in the *Norwich Chronicle* wrote that he 'had much to learn'. One was of his famous brother George. These were presumably in oil. The same critic praised a head in crayon. In the 1860 Exhibition he was represented by a portrait in water-colour of Mackey the Norwich astronomer.

SELECT BIBLIOGRAPHY

The Norwich artists attracted writers early. There was a brief account of Crome by Allan Cunningham in the *Cabinet Gallery of Pictures* (1834). Four years later Dawson Turner wrote a memoir of Crome as an introduction to *Crome's Etchings* (1838), and he also referred to him in his *Outlines of Lithography* (1840). In 1876 there was a reprint of a series of extracts from the *Norwich Mercury* of November and December 1858 by John Wodderspoon which also included a reprint of Dawson Turner's *Memoir*; this 1876 edition is referred to as the second but I have not come across the first. Theobald assumes that the first was published in 1858 but this is unlikely as the last *Mercury* extract is from December in that year. In 1860 *A Reverie* by David Hogdson marked the Loan Exhibition of that year and also at about this time appeared an undated monograph of E. T. Daniell by F. R. Beecheno. The *Portfolio* of 1879 contained a sketch of Crome's life by Mrs Charles W. Heaton. In 1897 the *Portfolio Artistic Monographs* series contained *John Crome and John Sell Cotman* by Laurence Binyon. *The Norwich School of Painting* by W. F. Dickes appeared in 1905; it is a wordy work but a quarry of information. In 1906 Sir Henry Studdy Theobald published *Crome's Etchings* amongst which he mistakenly included some by John Berney Crome. Theobald referred to the *Life of Crome* by Cosmo Monkhouse in the *Dictionary of National Biography*; to an article by Elise Paget on Crome in the *Magazine of Art* for April 1882; to an article on 'Some Forgotten Etchers' in the *English Illustrated Magazine* of December 1883 by Sir Walter Armstrong; to an essay on 'Old Crome' by Frederick Wedmore in *Studies in English Art*, 2nd edition, 1876; as well as to the more significant publications. In 1903 The Studio in *Masters of English Landscape Painting* included 'J. S. Cotman' by Laurence Binyon. In 1920 The Studio also produced *The Norwich School* by H. M. Cundall and in 1923 *The Water Colour Drawings of John Sell Cotman* with a commentary by A. P. Oppé. In 1921 C. H. Collins Baker's *Crome* became the fullest monographic treatment of the subject. His canon is not accepted but it provides the inevitable basis for further work on Crome although it is hopelessly inadequate on his watercolours. *John Crome* by S. C. Kaines Smith in 1923 tried to link Crome with Velasquez. In 1925–6 the Walpole Society published *John Sell Cotman's Letters from Normandy*, edited by H. Isherwood Kay. This activity in the interest of Cotman resulted in 1937 in a full-length *Life of John Sell Cotman* by Sidney D. Kitson which, despite some weakness such as misquotation and, inevitably, some mistakes in dating, is unlikely to be superseded. This was followed in 1953 by *John Sell Cotman 1782–1842* by Victor Rienacker with some good illustrations. In 1961 appeared *Old Norwich, A Collection of Paintings, Prints and Drawings*, compiled by Alec M. Cotman and Francis W. Hawcroft, which is particularly rich in illustrations of the topographical work of the School. Several volumes of the *Walker Gallery Quarterlies* deal with members of the School.

In addition to these there are references, more or less illuminating, in all general works on English nineteenth-century landscape painting and in books upon water-colour in particular; in S. L. Roget's *History of the Old Water Colour Society*; in Redgrave's *Century of British Painters*; in Hughes's *Early English Water Colour*; in Iolo Williams's *Early English Water Colours*; in the *Victoria and Albert Museum Catalogue* and its *Appendix*; and in others besides.

The most extensive collection of ephemeral publications, Norwich Society Exhibition catalogues and the like, together with much manuscript material, is naturally in Norwich Castle and the Norwich City Library. The British Museum is, however, the repository of the documents and notes collected and made by James Reeve over a lifetime's study of the School. This *cache* has provided the basis for much of the subsequent biographical work.

The books most frequently referred to in the text have been abbreviated as follows:

The Norwich School of Painting by W. F. Dickes (Dickes).

The Norwich School by H. M. Cundall (Cundall).

The Water Colour Drawings of John Sell Cotman by A. P. Oppé (Oppé).

Crome by C. H. Collins Baker (Collins Baker).

John Sell Cotman by Sidney D. Kitson (Kitson).

Old Norwich, A Collection of Paintings, Prints and Drawings compiled by Alec M. Cotman and Francis W. Hawcroft (Cot. and Haw.).

The Plates

1a. John Ninham (1754–1817) *A View of Norwich*

1b. Attributed to Charles Catton R.A. (1728–1798) *View of the Bridges at Hawick*

2a. Charles Catton Jr. (1756–1819) *A View of Norwich*

2b. William Capon (1757–1827) *The Entrance to the Opera House*

3a. William Williams (fl. 1758–1795) *Vagrants with a Donkey*

3b. William Williams (fl. 1758–1795) *Loading a Pack Donkey*

4a. James Sillett (1764–1840) *Black Grapes*

4b. James Sillett (1764–1840) *The Old Oak at Winfarthing*

5a. Attributed to James Sillett (1764–1840) *Bishop's Bridge*

5b. Charles Hodgson (fl. 1797) *River Scene*

6a. John Crome (1768–1821) *Near Lakenham*

6b. John Crome (1768–1821) *Patterdale*

7b. John Crome (1768–1821) *By the Roadside*

7a. John Crome (1768–1821) *Tintern Abbey*

8a. John Crome (1768–1821) *Mountainous Landscape*

8b. John Crome (1768–1821) *Trees on a Bank*

9a. John Crome (1768–1821) *The River through the Trees*

9b. John Crome (1768–1821) *The Sunken Lane*

10b. John Crome (1768–1821) *Blacksmith's Shop at Hingham*

10a. John Crome (1768–1821) *Entrance to Earlham Park*

11b. John Crome (1768–1821) *The Glade Cottage*

11a. John Crome (1768–1821) *The Blasted Oak*

13. John Crome (1768–1821) *Houses and Wherries on the Wensum*

12. John Crome (1768–1821) *Wood Scene*

14a. John Crome (1768–1821) *Silver Birches: after Pynaecker*

14b. John Crome (1768–1821) *Trees by Water: after Cuyp*

15a. Attributed to Robert Ladbrooke (1770–1842) *The Waggoner and Oak*

15b. Robert Ladbrooke (1770–1842) *Norfolk Broad, Evening*

16. Robert Ladbrooke (1770–1842) *A Forge by Moonlight*

17b. John Thirtle (1777–1859) *The Harvester's Family*

17a. Robert Ladbrooke (1770–1842) *Glymlffes Bridge*

18a. John Thirtle (1777–1839) *Beached Fishing Boat*

18b. John Thirtle (1777–1839) *Thorpe Staithe*

19a. John Thirtle (1777–1839) *Tombland, Norwich*

19b. John Thirtle (1777–1839) *River Scene near Norwich*

20. John Thirtle (1777–1839) *View over a Plain*

21a. Edwin W. Cooper (fl. 1803–1831) *A Piebald Horse and a Dog in a Landscape*

21b. Edwin W. Cooper (fl. 1803–1831) *A House in a Park*

22a. J. Gooch (fl. 1797–1823) *Beaudesert*

22b. J. Gooch (fl. 1797–1823) *Old Carrow Bridge*

23a. Major-General James Pattison Cockburn (1779–1849) *Cavalry Barracks, Norwich*

23b. Robert Dixon (1780–1815) *Cottage Scene*

24a. Robert Dixon (1780–1815) *Village Windmill*

24b. Robert Dixon (1780–1815) *The Mill at Cromer*

25a. Robert Dixon (1780–1815) *Fishermen's Cottages*

25b. Robert Dixon (1780–1815) *Beeston Hill, Sheringham in the Distance*

26b. Francis Stevens (1781–1825) *House at Wortley, near Sheffield*

26a. Paul Sandby Munn (1775–1845) *Mill on the Vale of Rhyddel*

27a. Francis Stevens (1781–1823) *Near Beccles, Suffolk*

27b. Attributed to David Cox (1783–1859) *Evening Landscape*

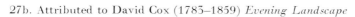

28a. John Sell Cotman (1782–1842) *Cottage near Guildford Churchyard*

28b. John Sell Cotman (1782–1842) *Brecknock*

29a. John Sell Cotman (1782–1842) *Barmouth Estuary*

29b. John Sell Cotman (1782–1842) *Bedlam Furnace*

30b. John Sell Cotman (1782–1842) *Study of Trees, Harrow*

30a. John Sell Cotman (1782–1842) *An Overshot Mill*

51b. John Sell Cotman (1782–1842) *Ancient Bath, Composition*

51a. John Sell Cotman (1782–1842) *Devil's Elbow, Rokeby Park*

52b. John Sell Cotman (1782–1842) *The Marl Pit*

52a. John Sell Cotman (1782–1842) *The Mars off Cromer*

33a. John Sell Cotman (1782–1842) *St. Botolph's Priory, Colchester*

33b. John Sell Cotman (1782–1842) *Cottages, Elm Hill, Norwich*

34a. John Sell Cotman (1782–1842) *A Castle*

34b. John Sell Cotman (1782–1842) *St. Paul's from the River*

35a. John Sell Cotman (1782–1842) *Boston Church, Lincs.*

35b. John Sell Cotman (1782–1842) *Coutances*

36a. John Sell Cotman (1782–1842) *Abbatial House of St. Ouen, Rouen*

36b. John Sell Cotman (1782–1842) *Snowdon*

37a. John Sell Cotman (1782–1842) *Mills at Crowland*

37b. John Sell Cotman (1782–1842) *A Draining Mill*

38a. John Sell Cotman (1782–1842) *Storm on Yarmouth Beach*

38b. John Sell Cotman (1782–1842) *The Story of Bathsheba*

39a. John Sell Cotman (1782–1842) *Via Mala*

39b. John Sell Cotman (1782–1842) *The Wind in the Trees*

40a. John Sell Cotman (1782–1842) *Mountain Landscape*

40b. John Sell Cotman (1782–1842) *Trees on a Hill*

41a. David Cox (1783–1859) *The Windmill*

41b. Attributed to Edmund Girling (1796–1871) or Richard Girling (1799–1862) *Cumberland*

42a. Henry Ninham (1793–1874)
St. Andrew's, Norwich

42b. Henry Ninham (1793–1874)
A Thatched Cottage

43a. John Berney Crome (1794–1842) *Yarmouth Beach with Windmills*

43b. John Berney Crome (1794–1842) *Yarmouth Beach,* 1840

44a. James Stark (1794–1859) *In the Isle of Purbeck*

44b. James Stark (1794–1859) *Eton College*

45a. James Stark (1794–1859) *Sandhills on the Coast*

45b. James Stark (1794–1859) *Cottages*

46a. James Stark (1794–1859) *The Pasture Pond*

46b. James Stark (1794–1859) *Rocks and Trees*

47a. James Bulwer (1794–1879) *Near Clifton*

47b. James Bulwer (1794–1879) *Beeston Regis Church*

48a. George Vincent (1796–1832) *The Needles*

48b. George Vincent (1796–1832) *Shipping Scene*

49a. George Vincent (1796–1852) *In the Highlands*

49b. George Vincent (1796–1852) *Prospect from a Ruin*

50. Joseph Stannard (1797–1830) *Lugger in a Squall*

51a. Joseph Stannard (1797–1830) *Schooners in a Calm Sea*

51b. Joseph Stannard (1797–1830) *Hoisting the Sail*

52a. William Joy (1803–1867) and John Cantiloe Joy (1806–1866) *King George IV passing Great Ormesby, Yarmouth, on his return from Edinburgh, 1822*

52b. J. G. Zobell (1791–1879) *Sandling Ferry*

53a. David Hodgson (1798–1864) *Horstead Mills*

53b. David Hodgson (1798–1864) *Landscape with Trees*

54a. Thomas Churchyard (1798–1865) *The Moored Barge*

54b. Samuel David Colkett (1800–1863) *Cottage Scene*

55a. Samuel David Colkett (1800–1863) *The Track to the Field*

55b. Samuel David Colkett (1800–1863) *The Woodland Cottage*

56a. Robert Leman (1799–1863) *Cattle in a Pool*

56b. Robert Leman (1799–1863) *Trees*

57. Robert Leman (1799–1863) *The Water Gate*

58a. Robert Leman (1799–1863) *The Shepherd on the Heath*

58b. Robert Leman (1799–1863) *At Trowse*

59a. G. S. Stevenson (fl. 1830) *The Old Fishmarket*

59b. William Taylor (1800–1861) *Purfleet*

60a. Thomas Lound (1802–1861) *Gorleston Pier*

60b. Thomas Lound (1802–1861) *View of Norwich*

61a. Thomas Lound (1802–1861) *Boathouse on the Yare*

61b. Thomas Lound (1802–1861) *Cottages at East Barsham*

62a. Thomas Lound (1802–1861) *St. Benet's Abbey*

62b. John Berney Ladbrooke (1803–1879) *Below Beddgelert*

63a. John Berney Ladbrooke (1803–1879) *View in Snowdonia*

63b. John Berney Ladbrooke (1803–1879) *The Team at the Bridge*

64a. Obadiah Short (1803–1886) *Norwich from Mousehold*

64b. Edward Thomas Daniell (1804–1842) *River Scene*

65a. Edward Thomas Daniell (1804–1842) *Stormy Sunset*

65b. Edward Thomas Daniell (1804–1842) *Near Kalabshee*

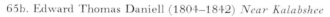

66. Edward Thomas Daniell (1804–1842) *El Fatha, Sinai*

67a. William Howes Hunt (1807–1879) *Yarmouth*

67b. Alfred Priest (1810–1850) *River Scene*

68a. Joseph Geldart (1808–1882) *Landscape Composition*

68b. Joseph Geldart (1808–1882) *The Well*

69a. Miles Edmund Cotman (1810–1858)
Interior of a Barn

69b. Miles Edmund Cotman (1810–1858)
On the Banks of the Yare, Reedham

70a. Miles Edmund Cotman (1810–1858) *A River Bank*

70b. William Philip Barnes Freeman (1813–1897) *Breydon*

71a. William Philip Barnes Freeman (1813–1897) *The Village Pump*

71b. Henry Bright (1814–1873) *Sunset at Low Tide*

72a. Henry Bright (1814–1873) *Low Tide*

72b. Henry Bright (1814–1873) *The Windmill*

73a. Henry Bright (1814–1873) *Old Mill, Clovelly*

73b. John Joseph Cotman (1814–1878) *The Dolphin Inn, River Wensum*

74. John Joseph Cotman (1814–1878) *Foliage, late Summer*

75a. John Joseph Cotman (1814–1878) *On the Banks of the Stream*

75b. John Joseph Cotman (1814–1878) *A River Reach*

76a. John Joseph Cotman (1814–1878) *The Flint Wall*

76b. Henry Jutsum (1816–1869) *Boxley, Kent*

77a. Henry Baines (1823–1894) *Castle Rising*

77b. John Middleton (1827–1856) *Tonbridge*

78a. John Middleton (1827–1856) *Blofield*

78b. John Middleton (1827–1856) *Near Butterdale, Cumberland*

79a. John Middleton (1827–1856) *Leaves*

79b. John Middleton (1827–1856) *Study of Rocks*

80a. W. Rowland (fl. 1860) *North Quay and Townhall, Great Yarmouth*

80b. Harry Hine (fl. 1873) *A Surrey Mill*

Index

Abbatial House of St Ouen, Rouen; J. S. Cotman, 56; Pl. 36a
Ackerman, 24, 26, 29, 40
Adriatic, 71
Aegean, 71
alabaster, 4
Alby, Norfolk; J. Middleton, 76; Col. Pl. VIII
Alexander, William, 12
Alps, 11
Alva, 9 note 2
Ancient Bath, Composition; J. S. Cotman, Pl. 31b
Arcady, 7
Architectural Antiquities of Normandy, 40
art societies, 7
Asia Minor, 71
Associated Painters in Water-Colours, 34
At Trowse; R. Leman, Pl. 58b
Auricula from Nature, An; Mrs Frewer, 82
Aylsham, 62

Baines, Henry, 81
Baker, Collins, 87
Balliol, 50
Bardwell, Thomas, 15
Barker's of Bath, 7, 14, 17, 18, 82
Barmouth Estuary; J. S. Cotman, Pl. 29a
Barn; H. Bright, 76
Barrett, George, 56, 66
Bartlett, W. H., 85
Bath, 7, 10
Beached Fishing Boat; J. Thirtle, Pl. 18a
Beauchamps of Langley Hall, 11
Beaudesert; J. Gooch, Pl. 22a
Beaumont, Sir George, 31
Bedlam Furnace; J. S. Cotman, 29b

Beechey, Sir William, 84, 85, 87, 88
Beeston Castle; D. Cox, 67
Beeston Hill, Sheringham in the Distance; R. Dixon, Pl. 25b
Beeston Regis Church; J. Bulwer, Pl. 47b
Bell, E., 8, 81
Below Beddgelert; J. B. Crome, 44; Pl. 62b
Berchem, 9, 14
Berkeley, Mr, 81
Berney, Phoebe, 22
Birkbecks, 81
Birmingham, 7, 74 note
Bishop's Bridge; J. Sillett, Pl. 5a
Black Grapes; J. Sillett, Pl. 4a
Blacksmith's Shop at Hingham, The; J. Crome, 20; Pl. 10b
Blacksmith's Shop, Moonlight; R. Ladbrooke, 23
Blake, J., 18, 81
Blake, R., 81
Blake, William, 39, 50
Blasted Oak, The; J. Crome, Pl. 11a
Blenheim, battle of, 8
Blickling, 62
Blofield; J. Middleton, Pl. 78a
Blomefield, 47
Boathouse on the Yare at Reedham; T. Lound, 49; Pl. 61a
Bolton, 84
Bonington, R. P., 56, 65, 85
Borrow, George, 58
Borrow, John, 81, 88
Boston Church, Lincs.; J. S. Cotman, Pl. 35a
Both, Jan, 9
Boulevard des Italiens; J. Crome, 3
Bouquet, A. C., 6
Boxley, Kent; H. Jutsum, 76b
Boy Looking at a Bird; R. B. Joy, 51

Brandsby Hall, 30, 32
Brecknock; J. S. Cotman, Pl. 28b
Breydon; W. P. B. Freeman, Pl. 70b
Bright, Henry, 37, 48, 49, 52, 63, 67, 73, 75, 76, 79, 82
Brightwell, Miss, 36
Bristol, 1, 6
British Institution, The, 34, 41, 71, 82
Brittany, 84
Brown, Joseph, 15
Brown, Maria, 46
Browne, A., 18
Bulwer, Revd. A., 62 note
Bulwer, Henry, 62
Bulwer, Revd. J., 55, 57, 62, 68, 70
Bulwer Collection, 83
Burlington, End of, 8
Burrell, F. B., 81
Burrell, J. F., 81
Byron, Lord, 27
By the Roadside; J. Crome, 19; Pl. 7b

Callcott, Sir Augustines Wall, 85
Callow, William, 49, 78
Cambridge, 72, 82, 84
Camera lucida, 85, 86
Camera obscura, 86
Capon, William, 13, 25, 43
Carlisle, 60
Caracci, the, 88
Carrow Bridge; J. Gooch, 82
Castle, A.; J. S. Cotman, Pl. 34a
Castle of Mortain; J. S. Cotman, 53
Castle Rising; H. Baines, Pl. 77a
Cattermole, G., 65, 85
Cattermole, R., 85
Cattle in a Pool; R. Leman, 48; Pl. 56a

Catton, Charles, 13, 14, 15, 43
Cavalry Barracks, The; J. P. Cockburn, 47; Pl. 23a
Chalon's Sketching Society, 84
Chantrey, Sir Francis, 85
Chardin, 43
Charles II, 8
Chatelain, J. B. C., 8
Chepstow, 18, 22
Chichester, 51
China, 7
Chinese scroll painting, 21
Chislehurst, 83
Cholmeley, the, 30, 31, 32, 54
Christening Feast, The; Jan Steen, 11
church brasses, 6
Churchyard, Thomas, 46, 49, 50, 84
City of London School, 73
city states, 5
Claude (Lorraine), 9, 42
Clifton Suspension Bridge, 62
Clinch, G., 85
Clover, Joseph, 81
Cockburn, James Pattison, 47
Colkett, Samuel David, 49, 50, 61, 72, 82, 84
Colkett, Victoria, 82
Collis, William, 28
Colman Collection, 14, 85
Constable, John, 12, 15, 22, 27, 42, 50, 79, 82
Conway, 22
Conway Castle; by R. Leman, 48
Cooke, W. B., 47
Cooper, Edwin W., 82
Coppin, Daniel, 82
Coppin, Miss, 18, 45
Cornwall, 83
Cotman, Alfred, 65, 67
Cotman, Anne, 58, 65
Cotman's Circulating Library, 33, 34
Cotman, Francis Walter, 66, 67
Cotman, John Joseph, 1, 58, 59, 61, 63, 67, 70, 73, 74, 75
Cotman, John Sell, 3, 24–30, 33, 34, 35, 37–41, 43, 44, 45, 47–55, 57, 58, 59, 61, 63, 65–68, 70, 71, 72, 76, 78, 79, 83, 84, 85, 89
Cotman, Miles Edmund, 48, 52, 56, 57, 61, 63, 65, 67, 70, 73, 74, 75
Cottages at East Bercham, Norfolk; T. Lound, Pl. 61b

Cottage near Guildford Churchyard; J. S. Cotman, Pl. 28a
Cottage Door, The; T. Gainsborough, 11
Cottages, Elm Hill, Norwich; J. S. Cotman, Pl. 33b
Cottages; J. Stark, Pl. 45b
Cottages; J .Thirtle, 24
Cottages; J. Stark, Pl. 45b
Cottage Scene; S. D. Colkett, Pl. 34b
Cottage Scene; R. Dixon, Pl. 23b
Cottages on the Wensum; J. Crome, 42
Coutances; J. S. Cotman, Pl. 35b
Cow Tower, 28
Cox, David, 12, 49, 50, 56, 64, 67, 74, 79, 85
Cozens, Robert, 12, 43
Crace Collection, 13
Cristall, Joshua, 22, 29
Crome, Emily, 78, 82
Crome, Frederick, 78, 82
Crome, John, 1, 3, 4, 11, 12, 15–22, 24, 26, 28, 29, 33, 35–39, 41–46, 48, 49, 51, 52, 61, 66, 72, 79, 83, 84, 86–89
Crome, John Berney, 22, 35, 36, 37, 44, 48, 55, 60, 61, 63, 71, 78, 86, 89
Crome, William, 78, 82
Cromer, 23, 68
Crotch, Dr, 18
Cumberland, 19, 53, 84
Cumberland; E. Girling, Pl. 41b
Cupid Benighted; Robert Dixon, 26
Cuyp, 9, 11, 12, 41

Danby, the, 6
Daniell, Revd. E. T., 50, 51, 56, 71, 89
Daniells, the, 12
Dartmoor, 67
Day, Ellen, 47
Dayes, Edward, 16
Daylight; a recent Discussion etc.; by Henry Richter, 40
Deaths of Nelson, 27
de Loutherbourg, 10
Demolition of the Cathedral Infirmary; J. Crome, 20
Design for a Ceiling; Robert Dixon, 25
Despairing Lover; J. Thirtle, 24

Devil's Elbow, The; J. S. Cotman, 29; Pl. 31a
Devon, 83
de Wint, Peter, 12, 25, 31, 51, 61, 79
Dibden, T. C., 49
Dismantled Brig. The; John Sell Cotman, 70
Dixon, Robert, 18, 25, 26, 39, 72, 83
Dixon, Thomas, 25
Dolphin Inn, The River Wensum; J. J. Cotman, Pl. 73b
Donthorne, John, 82
Downman, John, 6, 24
Draining Mill, A; J. S. Cotman, 54; Pl. 37b
Dreadnought and Grampas, Hospital Ships on the Thames; M. E. Cotman, Col. Pl. V
Dropgate; J. S. Cotman, 76
Drury Lane, 13
Dulwich College Gallery, 41
Durer, 16, 20

East Anglian School of Illumination, 4, 5
Eastlake, Sir Charles, 7
Egypt, 7
El Fatha, Sinai; E. T. Daniell, Pl. 66
Elizabeth I, 8
Elliot, Captain R., 55
Embarkation of St Ursula; Tintoretto, 11
Englefield, Sir Henry, 31, 85
Entrance to Earlham Park; J. Crome, 20; Pl. 10a
Eton College; James Stark, Pl. 44b
Etty, William, 76, 81, 85
Evening Landscape; D. Cox, Pl. 27b
Evening Ride Near a River; Cuyp, 41
Exeter, 6, 85

Fisherman's Cottages, Onverstrand near Cromer; R. Dixon, Pl. 25a
Fleming, Williams Ian, 7 note
Flint Wall, The; J. J. Cotman, Pl. 76a
Flixton Hall; J. S. Cotman, 66, 67, 70
Florence, 73
Foliage, Late Summer; J. J. Cotman, Pl. 74

Index

Forge by Moonlight, A; R. Ladbrooke, Pl. 16
foreign travel, 12
France, 50
Freeman, J., 18
Freeman, Miss, 18
Freeman, William Philip Barnes, 73, 75, 82
French influence, 8, 9
Frewer, Mrs. 18, 82
Fripps, the, 6
Frith, 76
Frost, George, 16
Fry, Roger, 7, 8 note

Gainsborough, Thomas, 9–12, 15–17, 20, 21, 43, 88
Gastineau, Henry, 85
Gates of Norwich; J. Ninham, 84
Geldart, Joseph, 55, 57, 73, 81
Gendall, John, 6
George III, 13
Gibson, Mr, 18
Giles Le Flemming, 5
Gilpin family, 16, 22
Gilpin, William, 11
Giorgione, 9
Girling brothers, 52, 53
Girtin, Thomas, 15, 16, 19, 26, 27, 28, 30, 43, 67, 79
Glade Cottage; J. Crome, 20; Pl. 11b
glass painters, 5, 6
Glover, Miss, 47
Glover, William, 29
Glymllffes Bridge; Robert Ladbrooke, 23, Pl. 17a
Gooch, J., 82
Goodrich, 18
Gordon, The Revd. W., 18, 82
Gorleston Pier; T. Lound, Pl. 60a
Grand Tour, 11
Gravelot, 8
Greta Bridge; J. S. Cotman, 53, 69
Greta Woods drawings, 75, 77
Gurney family, 11, 16, 18, 19, 46, 54, 81

Hannibal Crossing the Alps, 27
Hansell, Henry, 47
Hanworth, 68
Harbourne, 74 note
Harding, J. D., 47, 55, 79
Hardy, Henry, 6
Harriot, W. H., 55, 70

Harrison, C. H., 82
Harvest Time; J. Thirtle, Pl. 17b
Harvey, Thomas, 11, 16, 17, 41, 88
Harwin, W., 18
Havell, William, 56
Hawcroft, Francis, 41 note
Haydon, Benjamin, 84
Head of Laocoon; Robert Dixon, 26
Hearne, Thomas, 12
Henry VIII, 5, 7, 8
Hills, Robert, 84
Hine, Harry, 82
Hine, Mrs, 82
History of Norfolk; Blomefield, 47, 62
History of Somerset; Collinson, 62
Hobbema, 9, 11, 12, 16, 17, 41
Hockford Church; Maria Brown, 47
Hodges, William, 12
Hodgson, Charles, 18, 26, 33, 46, 51, 81
Hodgson, David, 46, 50, 60, 61, 62, 27, 89
Hogarth, William, 8
Hoisting the Sail; J. Stannard, Pl. 51b
Holbein, 8
Hole in the Wall, 4
Holland, 9, 45
Hollar, Wenceslaus, 12
Holloway, Thomas, 15
Holmes, Sir Charles, 87
Holne, 83
Horstead Mills; D. Hodgson, 53b
House at Wortley, near Sheffield; F. Stevens, Pl. 26b
House in a Park; E. Cooper, 21b
Houses and Wherries on the Wensum; J. Crome, 21, 38; Pl. 13
Hunt, William Harvey, 52 note
Hunt, William Henry, 52 note
Hunt, William Holman, 52 note
Hunt, William Howes, 52 note

Imitations of Bronze: Fobert Dixon, 26
Industrial Revolution, 71
Interior of a Barn; M. E. Cotman, Pl. 69a

Interior of Spruggin's Hall; J. S. Cotman, 65
In the Highlands; G. Vincent, Pl. 49a
In the Isle of Purbeck; J. Stark, Pl. 44a
Ireland, 50
Isle of Man, 83
Italian Opera House, 13
Italy, 9, 50

Jackson, Samuel, 6
Jacobs, Miss, 18
Jaggers of Norwich, 46
Jesus College, Cambridge, 62
Johnson, Dr Samuel, 48
Joy, John Cantiloe, 51, 52
Joy, William, 45, 51, 52
Jukes, F., 14
Jutsum, Henry, 78, 83

Keats, John, 76
Kent, 76
Kent, William, 8
King John and Prince Henry at Swineshead Abbey; J. S. Cotman, 65
King's College, 58, 61, 65, 70, 73
King's Lynn, 13, 81, 84
Kneller, Sir Godfrey, 8
Koninck, 9

Ladbrooke, John Berney, 22, 23, 44, 73, 75
Ladbrooke, Robert, 3, 16, 18, 22, 23, 26, 33, 39, 42, 44, 45, 51, 52, 60, 71, 82, 84
Lake District, 11, 18, 19
Lancashire, 84
Landscape Annuals, 55
Landscape Composition; J. Geldart, Pl. 68a
Landscape at Cortessey, Norfolk; O. Short, 50
Landscape Composition with the Story of Bathsheba; J. S. Cotman, Pl. 38b
Landscape—Evening; J. Varley, 53
Landscape near Domfront; J. S. Cotman, 53
Landscape with Sporting Dogs and Game; E. Cooper, 82
Landscape with Sheep; J. Gooch, 82
Landseer, Sir Edwin, 71, 81
Lawrence, Sir Thomas, 27
Lear, Edward, 79

Leeds, Master, 18
Leeds Society, 60
Leeds, W. C., 18
Leaves; J. Middleton, Pl. 79a
Lely, Sir Peter, 8
Leman, Robert, 48, 65, 76, 77
Lewis, F. C., 79
Linnell, John, 50, 85
Liverpool, 7, 10
Llangollen, 22
Llanrwst, 22
Loading a Pack Donkey; W. Williams, Pl. 3b
London, 9, 10, 12, 51, 60, 62, 65, 72, 73, 74, 77, 83, 86, 88
Louis XIV, 8
Lound, Thomas, 48, 49, 52, 61, 72, 75, 77
Love, Horace Beevor, 81
Low Tide; H. Bright, 64; Pl. 72
Lugger in a Squall; J. Stannard, 45; Pl. 50
Lullingstone, 77
Lynmouth, 67

Mackay, 87
Madeira, 62
Magdalen, after Guido, A; Mrs Frewer, 82
Manby, Captain G. W., 51
Manchester, 7, 10, 60
Marl Pit, The; J. S. Cotman, 33; Pl. 32b
Mars off Cromer, The; J. S. Cotman, Pl. 32a
Medway, 67
Middle Ages, 5
Middleton, John, 37, 48, 65, 72, 75, 76, 77, 82
Middleton Tower, Norfolk; J. S. Cotman, 57
Miles, Edward, 15
Military College, Sandhurst, 83
Mills at Crowland; J. S. Cotman, 54; Pl. 37a
Mill, The; Rembrandt, 36
Mill, Eye, Suffolk, The; J. S. Cotman, Col. Pl. III
Mill on the Vale of Rhyddal, Cardiganshire; P. S. Munn, 26a
Mill Wheel, The; J. Crome, 19, 20; Col. Pl. I
Monro, Dr T., 16, 26, 29
Mont, St Michel; J. S. Cotman, 53, 56, 65
Moonlight, A; J. B. Crome, 19, 20, 61

Moored Barge, The; T. Churchyard, Pl. 54a
Morland, George, 14
Mortlock, 83
Mountain Landscape; J. S. Cotman, Pl. 40a
Mountain Scene; J. S. Cotman, 67
Mountainous Landscape; J. Crome, 19; Pl. 8a
Moushold, 50
Mulready, 71
Müller, William, 6, 56, 57, 76, 79
Munn, Paul Sandby, 30, 69, 83
Muskett, 84

Naples, 84
Napoleonic Wars, 22
Nash, 65
National Gallery, 84
Near Beccles, Suffolk; F. Stevens, Pl. 27a
Near Butterdale, Cumberland; J. Middleton, 77; Pl. 78b
Near Carrow Bridge; R. Ladbrooke, 23
Near Clifton: J. Bulwer, Pl. 47a
Near Kalabshee; A. T. Daniell, Pl. 65b
Near Lakenham; J. Crome, 19, 38, Pl. 6a
Near Magdalen Gates; R. Dixon, 25
Needles from Christchurch, The; G. Vincent, 37, 38, 44; Pl. 48a
Needles, The; J. S. Cotman, 53, 70
Netherlands, 6, 8, 9
Newcastle, 7, 60
Newmarket, 82
New Society of Painters in Water-Colour, 63, 64, 82
Ninham, Henry, 35, 61, 71, 82
Ninham, John, 12, 13, 43, 60, 61, 84
Norfolk and Norwich Art Union, 72
Norfolk and Suffolk Institution for Promotion of Fine Arts, 60, 78
Norfolk and Suffolk Society, 50
Norfolk Broad, A; R. Ladbrooke, 26; Pl. 15b
Normandy, 40, 85
North Quay and Town Hall,

Great Yarmouth; W. Rowland, 83; Pl. 80a
North Walsham, 73
Norwich Amateur Club, 48
Norwich from the South East; J. Ninham, 12
Norwich Grammar School, 46, 50, 61
Norwich School of Design, 84
Norwich Society, 1, 3, 42, 44, 45, 51, 71, 75, 82, 83, 84
Nottingham, 4, 7
Nymph Bathing, A.; J. Thirtle, 24

Old Barn; H. Bright, 76
Old Barn, Kent; H. Bright, 64; Col. Pl. VI
Old Carrow Bridge; J. Gooch, Pl. 22b
Old Mill, Clovelly, Devon; H. Bright, 64; Pl. 73a
Old Oak at Winfarthing: J. Sillett, 13; Pl. 4b
Old Fishmarket, The; G. S. Stevenson, Pl. 59a
Old Waterside Cottages, Norwich; J. Thirtle, 38
On the Banks of the Stream; J. J. Cotman, Pl. 75a
On the Bank of the Yare, Reedham; M. E. S. Cotman, Pl. 69b
On the Coast; R. Ladbrooke, 25
On the Ramparts, Domfront; J. S. Cotman, 56
Opera House in the Haymarket; W. Capon, 13; Pl. 2b
Ostade, 16
Overshot Mill, An; J. S. Cotman, 32; Pl. 30a
Oxford, 1, 7, 50

Palestine, 71
Palmer, Samuel, 39, 50, 75
pargetting, 4
Paris, 82
Pars, William, 12
Pasture Pond, The; J. Stark, Pl. 46a
Patience, J., 83
Patterdale, Sketch in; J. Crome, 19; Pl. 6b
Patterson, John, 11
Peak District, 18, 19
Pearson, William, 7
Pencil Studies after Crome; J. Stark, 36

Percy, J., 18

Persner, Professor, 4 note, 70 note

Picturesque Normandy; J. S. Cotman, 41

Piebald Horse and a Dog in a Landscape; E. Cooper, 21a

Piercefield, 18

Piranesi, 68

Place, Francis, 6

Plymouth, 83

Pococks, the, 6

population, 10

Portsmouth, 51

Portugal, 62

Poussin, Gaspard, 11, 29, 68

Pre-Raphaelite Circle, 63

Priest Alfred, 61, 73

Prospect from a Ruin; G. Vincent, Pl. 49b

Prout, Samuel, 6, 49, 66, 70, 79, 84

provincial schools, 7

Pugin, A. W., 84

Purfleet; W. Taylor, 84; Pl. 59b

Putney, 51

Pynaecker, A., 41

Quakers, 11, 81

Raby Castle; F. Stevens, 84

Ramparts of Domfront; J. S. Cotman, 65

Ranelagh Gardens, 13

Red Books; H. Repton, 83

Reeve Collection, 37, 52

Reeve, James, 39, 75, 85

Reinagle, R. R., 84

Rembrandt, 4, 9, 32

Repton, Humphrey, 83

Reverie, A; D. Hodgson, 72

Reynolds, Sir Joshua, 15, 86

Rhineland, 64

Richter, Henry, 40

Richmond; J. Middleton, 77

Rigby, Dr, 4, 15, 16

Ripon, 7

River Bank, A; M. E. Cotman, Pl. 70a

River Landscape; J .J. Cotman, Col. Pl. VII

River Reach, A; J. J. Cotman, Pl. 75b

River through the Trees, The; J. Crome, 19; Pl 9a

River Scene; E. T. Daniell, Pl. 64b

River Scene: C. Hodgson, Pl. 5b

River Scene; A. Priest, Pl. 67b

River Scene Near Norwich; J. Thirtle, Pl. 19b

Roberts, David, 55, 71

Robertson, James, 7

Robson, George Fennel, 25, 47, 56, 64

Rocks and Trees; J. Stark, Pl. 46b

Rokeby Park, 31

Romanticism, 27

Romantic Revival, 1

Rome, 84, 88

Rooker, Michel 'Angelo', 14

Rosa Salvator, 9, 11, 22, 68

Rossetti, Dante Gabriel, 65

Royal Academy, The, 13, 14, 15, 22, 25, 28, 36, 71, 87

Royal Academy Schools, The, 72

Rowbotham, the, 7

Rowbotham, T. L., 78

Rowland, W., 83

Rubens, 75, 86

Ruined Castle on a Moonlit Crag; H. Bright, 64

Ruskin, J., 79

Ruysdaal, S., 9, 12, 17, 42

St Andrew's, Norwich 1848; H. Ninham, Pl. 42a

St Benets' Abbey, 52

St Benets' Abbey; T. Lound, Pl. 62a

St Botolph's Priory, Colchester; J. S. Cotman, 33a

St Mary Redcliffe, 62

St Paul's from the River; J. S. Cotman, Pl. 34b

St Paul's South Audley Street, 71

St Peter Mancroft, 25, 82

Sandhills on the Coast at Winterton, Norfolk; J. Stark, Pl. 45a

Sandling Ferry; R. Ladbrooke, 23, 37, 84

Sandling Ferry; J. G. Zobell, 84; Pl. 52b

Sandys, A. F. A., 62

Sandys, Frederick, 62

Saxmundham, 63

Scenery of the Rivers of Norfolk; J. Stark, 72

Schooners in a Calm Sea; J. Stannard, 45; Pl. 51a

Scotland, 11, 38, 50, 64

Scott, Sir Walter, 27

Set Piece, Body Colour; R.

Ladbrooke, 22

Severn Valley, 18

Shadowed Stream, The; J. S. Cotman, 76

Sharp, Michael, 83

Shee, Sir Martin, 10, 84

Shelly, Arthur, 83

Shelly, John William, 83

Shelly, Samuel, 83

Shepherd, The; J. S. Cotman, 67

Shepherd on the Heath, The; R. Leman, Pl. 58a

Sheringham, 68

Short, Obadiah, 50, 73; Pl. 64a

Shropshire, 4

Sillett, James, 13, 36, 42, 71

Silver Birches; after Pynaecker; J. Crome, 21, 24; Pl. 14a

Sketch Club, The, 28, 84

Sketches in the Style of Gainsborough; J. Crome, 20

Slate Quarries; J. Crome, 3

Smith 'of Derby', Thomas, 7

Smiths 'of Chichester', the, 7

Snowdon from Capel Curig; R. Leman, 48, 77; Col. Pl. IV

Snowdon with the Lake of Llanberis; J. S. Cotman, 54; Pl. 36b

Soane, Sir John, 70 and note

Society of British Artists, The, 37

Somerset, 62

Southport, 84

Speculative Society, The, 3

Squire, Paul, 63

Stafford, Marquess of, 31

Stanfield, W. Clarkson, 85

Stannard, Alfred, 46

Stannard, Joseph, 37, 45, 46, 48, 49, 50, 61, 75

Stark, A. J., 72

Stark, James, 14, 17, 36, 37, 45, 46, 50, 60, 61, 65, 71, 72, 73, 78, 87

Steen, Jan., 11

Steer, Wilson, 78

Stevens, Francis, 83

Stevenson, G. S., 84

Stevenson, William, 15, 84

Stone, F., 18

Storer, Mr, 86

Storm on Yarmouth Beach; J. S. Cotman, 58, 63, 69; Pl. 38a

Stormy Sunset; E. T. Daniell, Pl. 65a

Study of Rocks; J. Middleton, Pl. 79b

Study of Trees, Harrow; J. S. Cotman, 69; Pl. 30b
Sunken Lane, The; J. Crome, 19; Pl. 9b
Sunset at Low Tide; H. Bright, 64; Pl. 71b
Surrey Mill, A; H. Hine, 82; Pl. 80a
Switzerland, 47, 50, 57

Taylor, W., 84
Taylor, W. H., 84
Tavener, William, 16
Team at the Bridge, The; J. B. Ladbrooke, 44; Pl. 63b
Teniers, 41
Thames, 67
Thatched Cottage, A; H. Ninham, 42b
thatching, 4
Thirtle, John, 18, 24, 25, 26, 33, 38, 42, 46, 47, 48, 49, 51, 60, 61, 70, 72, 79
Thorpe Staithe; J. Thirtle, Pl. 18b
Timber Yard and Norwich Cathedral from the North; J. Thirtle, Col. Pl. II
Tintern, 18, 20, 22
Tintern Abbey; J. B. Ladbrooke, 44
Tintern Abbey; J. Crome, 20, 38; Pl. 7a
Tintoretto, 11
'Toledo' Style, 69
Tombland, Norwich; J. Thirtle, Pl. 19a
Tonbridge; J. Middleton, Pl. 77b
Towne, Francis, 12, 30, 51
Track in the Field, The; S. D. Colkett, Pl. 55a
Trees; R. Leman, 48; Pl. 56b
Trees by Water; J. Crome, 21, 41; Pl. 14b
Trees on a Bank; J. Crome, 19; Pl. 8b
Trees on a Hill; J. S. Cotman; Pl. 40b
Tristram, Professor E. W., 5
Tonbridge, 77
Tonbridge; J. Middleton, 76
Tunbridge Wells, 77
Turner, Dawson, 11, 15, 18, 30, 34, 40, 41, 44, 47, 53, 54, 55, 58, 68, 78, 85, 89, 90
Turner, J. M. W., 15, 16, 17, 26, 43, 56, 64, 71
Turner, William 'of Oxford', 7
Twickenham, 82

Ullswater, 83

Vagrants with a Donkey; W. Williams, Pl. 3a
Valley of Früdegen; J. P. Cockburn, 47
Van der Neer, 17, 36
Van Dyck, 8, 16, 20, 88
Van Goyen, 9
Van Huysum, 13, 45
Varley, Cornelius, 85
Varley, John, 15, 30, 33, 50, 53, 55, 56, 79, 84
Varley's Graphic Telescope, 85
Velasquez, 42, 89
Venice, 73
Via Mala; J. S. Cotman, 57, 70; Pl. 39a
Views in Rome; W. B. Cooke, 47
View in Snowdonia; J. B. Ladbrooke, 44; Pl. 63a
Views of Cottages and Farmhouses in England and Wales, F. Stevens, 84
Views of the Gates of Norwich, J. Ninham, 12
Views of Norwich, C. Catton, Pl. 2a
View of Norwich, J. B. Crome, 36
View of Norwich, T. Lound, Pl. 60b
View of Norwich, J. Ninham, Pl. 1a
View on the Coast of Baiae, R. Wilson, 11
View of the Bridges at Hawick, C. Catton, Pl. 1b
View of Wales, J. Varley, 53
View over a Plain; J. Thirtle, Pl. 20
Village Pump, The; W. P. B. Freeman, Pl. 71a
Village Windmill, R. Dixon, Pl. 24a
Vincent, George, 37, 38, 44, 45, 49, 61, 86

Waggoner and Oak; R. Ladbrooke, 23; Pl. 15a
Wales, 11, 18, 19, 22, 54, 64, 84
Waley, Arthur, 7
Walker, J. W., 84
wall-paintings, 5
Walpole, Horace, 86
Water-Colour Society, The, 31, 33, 56, 83
Waterloo, 52
Water-Gate, The; R. Leman, 76; Pl. 57

Water-Mill, The; J. S. Cotman, 28
Watteau, 45, 76
Well, The; J. Geldart, Pl. 68a
Welsh Cottages; John Thirtle, 24
West, B., 86
Westhall, R., 24, 39
Whisler, Francis, 15, 17
White, 16
Whitlingham; J. Crome, 19
Wilkins, William, 25, 84
Williams, Iolo, 16, 19
Williams, William, 14
Wilson, Richard, 10, 11, 12, 15, 17, 21, 43
Wiltshire, 4
Wind in the Trees; J. S. Cotman, Pl. 39b
Windmill, A; J. Thirtle, 24
Windmill, The; D. Cox, Pl. 41a
Windmill by a River; H. Bright, 64; Pl. 72b
Windsor, 83
Winter, C. J., 62, 83
Winter, Rowland, 83
Wollaston, Dr. W. H., 85
Woodforde, Dr., 5, 6
Woodland Cottage; S. D. Colkett, Pl. 55b
Woodland Landscape; J. Crome, 42
Wood Scene; J. Crome, 20, 38, 43; Pl. 12a
Woolwich, 67
Worcester, 81
Wordsworth, William, 28, 79
Wortley, 83
Wouverman, 86
Wreck of the Houghton Pictures; J. S. Cotman, 66, 67
Wright 'of Derby', 7
Wroxham Regatta; J. Crome, 41
Wye, 18, 19, 20

Yare, 61
Yarmouth, 11, 30, 34, 35, 36, 37, 39, 41, 51, 52, 53, 61, 68, 71, 72, 82, 84
Yarmouth; W. H. Hunt, Pl. 67a
Yarmouth Beach with Windmills; J. B. Crome, Pl. 43b
Yetts, W., 84
York, 6
Yorkshire, 30, 32, 53, 83
Yoxford, 83

Zobell, J. G., 84
Zuccarelli, 10